SEABEES & CROSSED BANANAS

Al Olser
CAPT, CEC, USN (Ret)

SEABEES & CROSSED BANANAS

by
Capt. A. N. Olsen
CEC, USN (Ret.)

— *Also by A. N. Olsen* —

THE KING BEE
A biography of Admiral Ben Moreell,
the founder of the U.S. Navy Seabees.

Copyright © 2011 by A. N. Olsen

ISBN-13: 978-0-9843585-9-5
ISBN-10: 0-9843585-9-5

Printed by Ag Press, 1531 Yuma, Manhattan, KS

Dedication

TO ALL SEABEE wives who have heard their husbands' sea stories time after time for years. They could probably repeat most of them word for word except for the fact that the story teller frequently has a tendency to embellish the tale as the years go by. Even so, the patience and understanding of Seabee wives is unsurpassed. Without their running things on the home front during frequent deployments and keeping everything intact, the troops in the field would not be nearly as effective. We all know SWSS!*

*Seabee Wives are Something Special.

Contents

Dedication		v
Book Title		ix
Preface		xi
I	Pete And The Major	1
II	The Brown Bombers	4
III	The Rat	7
IV	This Office Is Dirty	10
V	Hi Dozo	12
VI	Free Drinks	15
VII	Blomster Til Mor	19
VIII	Med Cap	23
IX	Embassy Duty	29
X	Shower With Mays	31
XI	The Washeteria	33
XII	Gamma Globulin	38
XIII	English Proficiency	41
XIV	Relieve The Pain	44
XV	Typhoon Condition One	47
XVI	The Tonsorial Parlor	51
XVII	Dynamite	54
XVIII	Such A Deal	58

XIX	Browning	62
XX	Belgian Beer	67
XXI	When Ya Gonna Make Chief?	70
XXII	Master Builder Test	74
XXIII	The Da Nang Dog	78
XXIV	You're A Yank Ain't Cha?	84
XXV	Purple Heart	88
XXVI	Religious Services	93
XXVII	Anchor Pool	95
XXVIII	Diego Shore Patrol	99
XXIX	Heir Apparent	102
XXX	Have A Beer In Bonn	106
XXXI	Seabee Betty	109
XXXII	What Happened To The Ape?	113
XXXIII	Whilst	117
XXXIV	Good Soup	120
XXXV	Sleeping On Watch	124
XXXVI	Letter From Momma	130
XXXVII	Kami Kaze	134
XXXVIII	This Island Sucks	137
XXXIX	Hello Seabee	141
XL	Ringnes Beer	149
XLI	Greens	153
XLII	The Marines Ain't So Bad	156
XLIII	Air Medals	159
XLIV	Torremolinos	164
XLV	Merry Christmas	167
XLVI	Tabacaleras	170
XLVII	Wardroom Dinners	176
XLVIII	Østeràs	182
XLIX	Send A Driver	187
L	Mel	190
LI	Seabee Sayings	193

Acknowledgements 195
Index 197
About the Author 200

Book Title

THE BOOK TITLE: "Seabees and Crossed Bananas" is probably a foreign phrase to everyone except the Seabees, the Civil Engineer Corps officers and some Navy and Marine Corps individuals who have been supported by Seabee battalions. I need to point out that everyone assigned to a Seabee unit is a Seabee. The title is not restricted just to the Group VIII construction ratings. All of the fleet rates such as yeoman, storekeeper, corpsman, etc. as well as the officers: Doctors, Dentists, Chaplains and Supply Corps Officers are considered to be Seabees once they have had battalion duty. Even our Marine Corps Gunny, who is assigned for military training, is a Seabee. Initially they usually show some resistance to accepting the Seabee connotation but by the time their tour is over they all seem to be quick to state they are Marines — but also Seabees.

Presuming that the casual reader does have some familiarity with the Navy's construction force known as the Seabees let me concentrate on the phrase "crossed bananas". In the U.S. Navy officers of the line wear a star on the cuff of their dress uniform to denote that designation. These are the officers who drive ships and submarines and fly and crash airplanes. Those of us in the staff corps refer to the line officers as members of the "line corps". Naturally no line officer agrees with us. And admittedly they are the officers who run the Navy. On the other hand those of us in the staff corps rather like our special niche and the ability to work in our chosen field, be it doctor, dentist, chaplain, supply or in my case the Civil Engineer Corps.

Just so there is no confusion over the separation between line and staff, each staff corps discipline is represented by a specific corps device which we wear on our cuff, or collar. Most all staff corps insignias are made up of some configuration using oak leaves and acorns. Due to the wide variety of oaks the leaf patterns are quite diverse. In the case of the Civil Engineer Corps the design is meant to replicate two drawing compasses, with the legs extended and overlapped and the adjusting screws up. The legs are represented by leaves of the quercus phellos variety of oak which produces long slender leaves. The adjusting screws are represented by acorns. The long slender oak leaves used for the CEC device are quite different from those used by doctors, dentists, nurses, etc. which are the more common oak leaf shape. At any rate the actual CEC device does have some resemblance to four interlaced, or crossed, bananas. Those of us in the Navy's Civil Engineer Corps have long ago accepted the sobriquet of "crossed bananas" to signify our collar device. And while most all of these stories deal with Seabees some include the battalion officers as well as pure CEC related sea stories. That's how the crossed bananas got into the title.

Preface

SEA STORIES SEEM TO have always been around. The first ones probably emerging after Noah made landfall on Mount Ararat. And sailors the world over have kept the supply of such stories coming year after year. The U.S. Navy certainly provides a good number of them, and the Seabees have generated their share. Based on my numerous Seabee tours over a 30 year career I can vouch for the fact that Seabee stories can compete with the best of them. Some are sad, most are funny and some can really curl your hair. And the best part is that there is a constant supply of source material for these tales, practically all of which are based on some particular incident. How that incident is portrayed in the story is sometimes questionable. Some are perfectly valid, some are embellished a good bit and others are an out-and-out lie. But they all began as an actual occurrence. Even so, it is often difficult to sort out just which category the sea story falls into. As Admiral Ben Moreell once said, "It is sometimes necessary to remember events which never occurred."

To reiterate, all the stories are based upon some actual occurrence. In some cases the name, or nickname, of the individual is the actual name. In a few instances the name has been changed to protect "the guilty bastard."

This collection of sea-stories encompasses my active duty time in the Navy which includes the Viet Nam period. Since then the Seabees have seen many other places around the world and I feel sure they are accumulating even more stories that will amaze and entertain anyone willing to listen.

As is frequently stated fairy tales begin with — "Once upon a time —" but sea stories start out with "Now this is no shit —." Well, stand by, because these are sea stories.

A. N. Olsen
Manhattan, Kansas

Chapter I

Pete and the Major

*I*N THE EARLY 60'S Okinawa was still recovering from the effects of WWII. The island was governed by the U.S. and the federal government appointed a high commissioner who was an Army Lt. General. Military bases were scattered around the island. For the most part the Army, NAS Naha and the Air Force bases were concentrated in the southern half of the island, the more metropolitan area. The Seabees and the Marines were relegated to the "boondocks" or the northern half of the island. At the mid point there was a mixture of Army, Air Force, Seabee and Marine bases. MCB-NINE deployed to Camp Kinzer (later renamed Camp Shields) in early '63. In those days the usual Seabee deployment site was whatever available spaces the local base commander could furnish. For the most part that consisted of decrepit facilities the base commander refused to use for any of his troops. Camp Kinzer was different. It was a complete Seabee camp. We were the hosts and not the tenants. It did not make any difference that we did not have any tenants because it was our camp. Maybe the reference to a complete camp is a bit of an exaggeration but we still thought we were living the good life compared to other deployment site accommodations. In addition to our standard construction work load we were busy reworking our quonset huts to make them as comfortable as possible. Of course we had a lot of other camp projects as well since this was a camp the Marines had abandoned. Just that fact alone should give most people some idea of the condition of the place.

The Bravo company shops had the lead on most of the camp projects. The guy who provided the material, supplies and advice for a good bit of the work was BU2 "Pete" Peterson. Despite his name Pete was not a Swede but a Samoan. He was an older fellow, fairly stocky and solid as a rock. As was the case with a number of sailors he was an E5 with three hash marks and just about ready to add his fourth. The term "career second class" could be used in reference to Pete as well as a lot of other enlisted men in those days. Promotions were essentially frozen in many rates and the openings seemed to occur only when someone died or retired. Generally that "career second class" reference had little to do with a sailor's qualifications or ability. That was the case with Pete who was regarded as a competent builder and an excellent carpenter. He was also a rather quiet person who kept to himself. Being older than most of his fellow Seabees he didn't participate in much of their off duty diversions, i.e. chasing nasans, hitting the bars and hotchi bath parlors and drinking all the beer they could get their hands on.

In fact there was no need for Pete to do any of those activities since he already had a girl friend, and a "round eye" at that. It seems that Pete had met up with an Army WAC Major early in the deployment and the two of them had a good thing going. Word had it that the major was a lot like Pete in that she was older than her colleagues, had probably seen her last promotion and was even built like him. But the two of them enjoyed each other's company and that was all that mattered. During that time frame there was not much of a formal non-fraternization policy in the military but it was understood by one and all that such associations between officer and enlisted, just were not done. Never the less the two of them had somehow become acquainted and they managed to find time to spend together without generating any concerns. Of course, this took some planning on the part of both of them. As an enlisted man Pete was forbidden to enter any "O" club and the major probably refused to go to the Seabee EM club. Considering the circumstances that was not a bad decision for any female. Apparently their solution was to meet in a nearby local town, Koza, and retire to a quiet bar.

This was the setting for the event that resulted in Pete becoming a "legend in his own time", at least within MCB-NINE. The Story is a little unclear in some details. But it seems that Pete and his major girlfriend were enjoying themselves in one of the bars of Koza one evening when three young Marines, who had already had more than their share of booze came into the bar. Being the only other customers in the bar Pete and the major (who was in civilian clothes, as was Pete) soon became the object of the Marines comments. And the comments were none too flattering. After one particularly disparaging remark directed at the major, Pete confronted them and told them to "knock it off". After a brief ration of crap from the Marines and a further response from Pete, which was probably delivered in his usual direct manner, one of the Marines made a fatal error and pushed Pete. This was decidedly the wrong thing to do as Pete reacted a bit more forcefully. In no time at all the other two Marines jumped into the fray. Another dumb decision on their part. In short order all three young grunts were laying around the bar room battered and bleeding. Of course the bar also suffered considerably as a result of this Seabee-Marine activity and the bartender immediately put in a call to the RASPS (Ryukyuan Armed Service Police). They arrived quickly and initially attempted to place Pete under arrest. About that time the major stepped in, identified herself to the military police and explained what had happened. The result was that the Marines were taken into custody but Pete had to make a statement regarding the incident. This statement was enclosed with the RASP report and eventually forwarded to the battalion.

After receiving the incident report the Executive Officer called Pete in for a pre-mast hearing. Pete was close mouthed about things most of the time but he was even more so when it came to describing the event to the X.O. It soon became apparent that he was very apprehensive about any word of the fight becoming known around the battalion. The X.O. asked if he was concerned about his friendship with the major causing her some embarrassment. It turned out that Pete was not overly concerned about that point but rather wanted to avoid having the battalion doctor learn of his little episode with the Marines. After considerable prodding by the X.O. it was discovered that Pete was afraid the Doc would be very upset with him since a small accident in the carpenter shop earlier had resulted in Pete being given a light duty chit.

It was unfortunate that we did not have a battalion newspaper in those days. I can see the headline now: "SEABEE ON LIGHT DUTY CHIT WIPES OUT A BAR FULL OF MARINES"!

Chapter II

The Brown Bombers

HARRY BROWN HAS A big nose. He also has a big smile. He was also the senior Seabee Team OIC having been promoted to full Lieutenant halfway through his Viet Nam Seabee Team tour.

Harry also had several other unique characteristics. He was the only CEC officer I knew who was from Kentucky — "The home of beautiful horses and fast women," as he liked to say. And for some reason his team experienced more Viet Cong (VC) and North Viet Nam Army (NVA) attacks than any other team in country in 1968.

For the most part Seabee teams were not harassed by the VC and only rarely were they attacked directly. The mission of the teams was civic action construction. This consisted of rebuilding bridges, roads, schools, clinics/hospitals, wells, etc. throughout the country. As such these projects did not constitute a significant military threat. The teams were always favorably received by the residents in every province since their projects provided a definite plus for the community. Consequently attacks on Seabee teams by the VC would most always be counterproductive to them.

But there were exceptions.

And Seabee team 7402 in Lai Thieu was for sure an exception. Harry, Dave Betts, a West Point graduate and our State Dept. liaison from USAID, and I talked about this several times but we could not pin point any reason why 7402 was getting all this attention. None the

Chapter II

less they and their project sites seemed to be a favorite target of opportunity for the VC who roamed around that sector.

On the night of 7 Sept. their camp area was hit by mortar fire. Harry and his team quickly made it to their fighting holes and bunkers so no one was wounded on that occasion. And miraculously there was very little damage to facilities and none to the team's equipment. Even so, the Seabees weren't given to counting their blessings. They wanted revenge. And they wanted it right away. Specifically they wanted their own mortar and a good supply of HE (high explosive) rounds. Unfortunately the CBPAC detachment had no crew served weapons other than M-60 machine guns which were already in each team's allowance. After several contacts around Saigon we were still unable to come up with a mortar. In the meantime Harry and his chief, SWC Evans, had been scouring the local MACV sector. On 10 Sept. PN1 Metz and I went to Lai Thieu and talked with the sector advisor and got a "probably" promise on getting a mortar for the team. After the day's discussion with the sector folks Metz and I stayed overnight with the team. Fortunately everything was quiet that night. It took almost a month but Harry finally cumshawed three 81 mm mortars from the sector. The team had the mortars set in some well developed mortar pits when Senior Chief Hess and I visited on 3 Oct. The tubes had been zeroed in on some known avenues of approach, but not yet test fired. The mortars, base plates and ammo were all staged in alcoves off the firing pit and available for rapid set up and firing. Aiming stakes were in place. All the team needed was an excuse to start lobbing rounds out.

Now that the team was ready to retaliate it seemed as if the VC activity had evaporated. Quite possibly the VC knew about the teams recent improvement in their weapons capability and decided not to force the issue. In any case the rest of Oct. and most of November passed without undue excitement for the Brown Bombers.

Then on 22 Nov. the team discovered five mines and booby traps around a bridge site project where they were working. After the team members found the mines they were removed by the district EOD crews before any job site activity. But obviously the team was in somebody's sights again.

We never did figure out exactly why Seabee Team 7402 had become such a target of opportunity for the VC. Their projects were the same as most other teams: roads, bridges, dispensaries etc., the team camp site had been in place for some time with no previous harassment. In fact 7402 was the third team to occupy the site. One theory offered up by some sector advisor officers seemed to be as logical as anything else. They suggested that the team camp was located very close to a recently developed VC infiltration route which was used to shuttle troops and supplies into Saigon from the northern areas. This was never proven conclusively but it made as much sense as any other idea. In any case we didn't have to wait much longer for some action. On the night of 5 Dec. the Lai Thieu camp site was hit with 12-14 mortar rounds. According to Harry's radio report by the time the first few rounds were landing his team had manned their mortar pits and were pumping rounds back out. A total of 32 outgoing rounds were fired and by that time all was quiet. According to Harry his team was really pumped up now. By their count a total of 52 rounds had hit the camp but only 32 had gone out. The Seabees were looking forward to not only catching up on the mortar count but actually pulling ahead in the total rounds comparison.

The team was due to be relieved in Dec. so they were concerned that they may not get the chance to catch up. I told Harry with the teams morale that high I may have to resort to burning their mail.

In spite of their becoming a neighbor-hood shooting gallery for the VC, no one on the team had been wounded in the mortar attacks. This was amazing considering the small area occupied by the team compound; i.e. something less than two acres.

One more brief mortar exchange took place the following night. Again the Seabees pumped out more rounds than they had incoming. But they were still slightly below on total count so their adrenalin level remained pretty high. Harry told me he was afraid some of his crew might not want to take the flight home until they had at least evened the score. Fortunately no one pressed the point.

Even though the Seabees managed to get through all the attacks unscathed it seems their firing was perhaps a bit more lethal. A patrol by the sector security the following morning reported one body — probably VC — in the area hit by mortars and blood around the area as well as other evidence of injured personnel. Obviously the teams protected mortar pits paid off both offensively and defensively.

Harry and "The Brown Bombers" left for Gulfport, Mississippi shortly after I departed for ConUS on 22 Dec. The last thing I did was draft a recommendation for a Meritorious Unit Commendation for the team. They certainly deserved it and perhaps even more. I never did find out if it was awarded. But Harry and his Brown Bombers can take a lot of satisfaction from the fact that they put some modern day emphasis into the "we fight" portion of the Seabee motto: "we build — we fight."

Chapter III

The Rat

MOST ALL AMERICANS who are of voting age can tell you exactly where they were on 9/11, 2001 when the muslim terrorists hit the world trade center towers and the Pentagon. Those of us who are now receiving monthly social security retirement checks can do the same with respect to 22 November 1963, the day President Kennedy was killed in Dallas.

In my case I was in Bangkok. But I am getting ahead of myself.

MCB-NINE deployed to Okinawa early in '63 and the Rat showed up on site shortly after we were there. A true southerner, a University of Alabama graduate, he had a typical southern drawl and he thought Bear Bryant was god. And he was a full lieutenant. Other than the doctor, dentist and the ops. officer all the junior officers were ensigns and jaygees. In fact the only CEC lieutenant billet in the battalion was that of the operations officer. Initially it made a bit of a problem for the command but it wasn't long before they slotted him in as Charlie Company Commander.

Where the Rat nickname came from I have no idea. He for sure didn't bring it with him but it became his handle very quickly. It wasn't meant to be derogatory, and he did not seem to mind the rest of the junior officers addressing him that way. But just to keep the few ensigns in place he frequently admonished them by saying: "That's Mr. Rat to you." In any case he quickly fit into the j.o. wardroom.

Near the end of our deployment the skipper announced he was sending some officers and chiefs to visit our Seabee team which was at that time deployed to Thailand. Two of our battalion senior chiefs had just been selected for promotion to E-9 (master chief) and they were named as well as the Rat and myself. The four of us caught space available hops to Thailand on resupply flights. The team was located in Warin about 300 miles northeast of Bangkok.

The team was principally involved in building a dam on one of the feeder rivers to the Mekong River — the main river in southeast Asia. The dam would enable the locals to control the water supply to their rice fields and allow them to have at least two and perhaps three rice crops per year. It was a pretty ambitious project for a team to attempt but now the job was nearly complete. It was an impressive piece of work.

Following our days in Warin we made our way back to Bangkok for the return flight to Okinawa. But first we had to sample the delights of Bangkok! After buying star sapphires at jewelry stores that served beer and also sold cobras, we bought Thai silk for some of the married officers to take back to their wives and then got on with the serious sightseeing. We toured many of the Wats (temples), rode the flat bottom boat in the klongs (canals) drank a lot of beer and eventually ended up at the La Cave restaurant in the Erawan hotel for dinner. I had a fantastic chateaubriand steak. Almost as good as the ones I am used to from the flint hills of Kansas. The only thing I was not able to work into the schedule was an opportunity to see some authentic Thai dancing. After dinner we made our way through a number of bars, where the dancing was definitely not traditional.

Seabee Sam our Thai driver, got us from place to place and eventually delivered us back to the hotel. Knowing I wanted to see some Thai dancing he offered to take me to the Thai cultural center the next morning to see the dancing but I would have to go very early, about 0600. We were scheduled to fly out at noon. That would not give me much sack time but after discussing the schedule timing, travel time to the airport, aircraft ETD, etc. I figured I could work it in and agreed to meet him then.

I was up early at the hotel the next morning showered, shaved and even had time to eat a bit of breakfast before Sam was due to arrive. This was 23 November in Bangkok as we were on the western side of the International Date Line. While I was in the hotel lobby I picked up an early edition of the Bangkok World (an English language newspaper) which contained the news of Kennedy's assassination in Dallas. This actually happened at about 0200 on the 23rd, Bangkok time.

At that point I forgot all about the Thai dancing exhibition (and I have never yet been able to observe a performance in person) and rushed

Chapter III

upstairs to pass the news to the Rat. I had to really beat on his door to wake him up but eventually I managed to do so. As soon as he opened the door he staggered back to his bed and collapsed. He seemed to be a bit groggy yet, or maybe just hung over but in either case he was not all that communicative. And I wanted to make sure he was at least alert enough that he could comprehend and assimilate what I was about to tell him.

We passed words back and forth for a short while and eventually the Rat sat up in bed and said something like: "Yeah I'm awake, what the hell you going to tell me that is so important?" I told him I had just read in the paper that the president had been shot while in Dallas.

I got no response at all. The Rat just stared off into space. He did not appear to be ready to say anything. He had that "1000 yard stare" and was apparently thinking about what I had just told him.

I waited. After all, I was just a jaygee while he was a full lieutenant. He would probably come up with some deep thoughts and reasoning quite soon.

Finally he spoke. He said, "How clean to you suppose that gal was that I was with last night?"

First things first, I guess.

Chapter IV

This Office Is Dirty

PROBABLY THE BIGGEST benefit a Navy officer gets from an assignment to a joint staff is the realization of just how fortunate he is not to have been in the Army or Air Force. Marines, being part of the Navy Department, we can usually adapt with fairly easily — especially if you are a Navy Seabee and spend much of your time ashore supporting Marine units. On the other hand, I suppose the Army and Air Force say similar things about the Navy.

But to take things one step further and have not only a joint staff assignment but an international joint staff billet really makes things interesting. Such is the case with a NATO assignment. Of course on a NATO staff everyone speaks English — in many instances much better than the Americans — but getting used to the different uniforms and rank designations can be both mind boggling and time consuming. By the time you quit saluting that Frenchman with all the gold because you just found out he's a 3rd class petty officer you might be six months into the tour. Still it is quite a treat to work with the various nationalities and services.

There is one other aspect of NATO duty which tends to complicate things from time to time and that is the fact that the locations of the various Headquarters are staffed predominately with local nationals. Again, most of them are fluent in English but many of the host country facilities people, contractors, vendors etc. are not usually familiar or comfortable using English. Sometimes this is inconvenient

Chapter IV

but more often than not it frequently develops into a pretty humorous situation.

Such was the case when my boss in Oslo, a U.S. Army Colonel, came into his office early one morning and noticed that the cleaning crew had forgotten to clean his spaces. The trash cans were still full, dust was still on the blinds, the rug had not been vacuumed or floors mopped etc. He immediately told his Norwegian secretary Unni, a very conscientious and capable girl, that she should contact the camp commandant (sort of a Norwegian Public Works Officer) and ask him to get a cleaning crew up to his office right away since the area was filthy.

Unni placed the call immediately and after contacting the appropriate individual she began to explain the problem. Of course this conversation was in Norwegian. It's important to know that the Norwegian word for dirty is "skitten" with the k pronounced as "sh". Thus the word is pronounced as if it were written shitten in English. Toward the end of her conversation Unni closed with the phrase: ". . . det var skitten!"

At this point the colonel set up straight, raised his eyebrows and said: "Well Unni I'm not sure it was all that bad!"

Chapter V

Hi Dozo

OKINAWA IN THE EARLY '60's was still a pretty Spartan place. Practically everything had been built following the battle for the island in '45, but for the most part, things were best described as functional. That was particularly so regarding the island infrastructure: buildings, roadways, utilities etc. And the U.S. military facilities were pretty much the same. The Seabees had been building permanent reinforced concrete barracks for the Marines at Camp Hansen and Camp Schwab for years but our own camp was still a collection of quonset huts. Even so, we were overjoyed to be there.

It seemed as if the powers that be must have it in for MCB-NINE for years. Our only deployment sites were Midway Island and Adak Island. After shuffling between these two bumps in the ocean for several years we could have been happy to go most anywhere. But when we got the word our next deployment would be to Okinawa we could hardly believe it. Now we could forget about the gooney birds and williwaws and begin to look forward to nasans. For several years in a row our only VD entries in the monthly ops report happened when we were in home port in California. Now things were different. After being in liberty purgatory for so long we now had the opportunity to rack up some surprising VD statistics. Or so many of the Seabees thought. And for the most part they tried hard to at least make a good showing even if they did not set a new CBPAC record. But the girls in Okinawa were not the only attraction. There were all sorts of liberty opportunities not available on Midway or Adak. The Seabees could

Chapter V

now go into towns, eat at restaurants, visit bars even go shopping in the nearby towns. There were even a number of local cultural events conducted by the Okinawans but other than bull fights (one bull versus another was the Okinawa versions of a bull fight.) and the Oban festival I doubt that our Seabees got too involved in such entertainment. Even so, it was a far cry from the experience of the past so we made the most of it.

Actually our liberty runs were not all that hair raising but we did enjoy our time on the beach. Camp Kinser was a Marine camp abandoned by the Marine Corps and made available to the Seabees. So you quickly get some idea of the facilities we inherited. The Marines never get rid of anything if it has any value at all. But Kinser was several miles away from Koza, the nearest town, and the easiest way to get there was to catch a skoshi cab at the gate and ride through Kadena Air Base to their gate 2, which was right on the edge of Koza. After arrival at gate 2 Street our first stop was usually the Paris barber shop. The Paris was always busy. There were about a dozen cute young nasan "barberesses," as we called them, working there who gave great haircuts, soothing conversation and complementary massages after the haircut. Some of us thought it bordered on immoral. That's why we were there. And it did not make any difference if you just had a haircut two days ago, you could always get another. In fact, I don't ever recall having to tell any of my Seabees to get a haircut during the entire deployment.

After the haircut the next stop was usually one, or several, of the numerous bars in Koza. They were all populated with a good number of smiling, friendly nasans who made sure we kept drinking and buying them drinks as well (we paid for drinks but their glasses were probably just dark tea). Some of the places had dancing, all had bands or juke boxes. Once we had downed all the booze we could afford, or hold, the next stop was a hotsi bath. This provided a gentle and civilized way to sober up. Coming out of the hotsi bath most all Seabee officers made a stop at the Napoli coffee shop. This was not exactly a coffee shop, it was more like an oriental diner. It was run by two sisters, Uriko and Mariko, who seemed quite old to us at the time. They were maybe in their 40's. But they had lived through the battle for Okinawa. They were quite friendly to all their U.S. customers but I suspected they still held some latent resentment for Americans. This was particularly so when they mixed the wasabi powder and soy sauce for our shishimi. That stuff made the strongest horseradish seem like cream cheese. The raw fish, wasabi sauce and coffee were guaranteed to sober up the biggest boozers. At this point we usually found another skoshi cab and made our way back to Camp Kinser.

In spite of all the various diversions available on gate 2 Street it was pretty much agreed throughout the battalion that the hotsi bath was the highlight of the evening. As previously stated, most all of us were wearing a big "grinner" by the time we got to the bath house. In spite of our various stages of intoxication we all looked forward to achieving some level of sobriety at the hands, and feet, of the bath house girls. Most of them were young girls but a number of them obviously had been around for some time. But that's another story. The standard procedure was generally as follows: strip off and sit on a small stool in the middle of the room. The bathhouse nasan would wet you down by pouring warm water from pitchers, making sure you were completely drenched. You would then be washed by the nasan using soap and cloth or soap and a sponge. Following that she would rinse you off using the warm water pitcher method again. At this point you would step into a big tub full of really hot water. Somehow the nasans seemed to know just how hot they could make the water and not have us gai-genes (foreigners) refuse to get in. The usual practice was to lay in the tub with only your nose above the water, and stay soaking there until the water became cool or you had wrinkles in your butt — whichever came first. At that point you would get out and lay on a table while the nasan pounded and massaged your backside. Some of them, fortunately the smaller ones, would get onto the table and actually walk up and down on your back. The more talented ones could actually provide some extra massage — by wiggling their toes as they trod all over your back.

But it was the washing portion of the hotsi bath session that proved to be the most educational part of the entire process. Once you were stripped, sitting on the stool and wet down the washing procedure would begin. The hotsi-bath parlors were bona fide bath houses, not fronts for bordellos as some believed. And when the bath house nasans gave you a bath you were given a real bath. They washed all the crevices in your ears, used small scrub brushes to get your fingernails and even toenails clean and using a soapy wash cloth they gave you a power wash over almost 100% of your body.

I know what you are thinking and I'm about to get there.

Once the bath house nasans were finished with their washing they would soap up the wash cloth and then hand it to you saying "hi dozo." We all knew what this entailed. It was for you to wash your own privates. But we were none of us linguists. And it was some time later before we learned hi dozo meant please, and not "wash your own balls."

Chapter VI

Free Drinks

THE SEABEE TEAM EFFORT in South Viet Nam was a major element of the "hearts and minds" program of MACV and the State Department. One of the objectives of the program was to present the U.S. military in a favorable light to all the citizens of the country. Our civic action construction work went a long way toward achieving those aims. Typical team projects included construction of schools, clinics, roads, bridges, water wells and water distribution systems. Teams also installed saw-mill equipment, developed a concrete pre-cast yard for producing reinforced concrete pipes, constructed a two story reinforced concrete high school building and even built a 120 foot clear span suspension bridge. All team projects were developed with the objective of providing benefits to a large percentage of the local community. And for the most part that's exactly how it worked out.

The program began in 1963 with the deployment of four well drilling teams and two Seabee teams. At that time the Seabee teams had been asked to assist the Army Special Forces by providing construction support to establish A team camps in bandit country throughout South Viet Nam. By 1967, two years after the U.S. military had entered the country in force, the Seabee team program had expanded to seven teams which were deployed throughout the II, III & IV Corps areas. The Marines and Seabee battalions were then deployed in I Corps so there was no point in sending teams to that region.

I arrived in South Viet Nam for my second full tour in late '67, just at the time we were expanding the program up to 15 teams. The CBPAC Detachment in Saigon was the headquarters for the Seabee team program. In addition to receiving and deploying the new teams we had a policy of relocating teams from one province to another after a period of time. The usual evolution of a team would begin with an open arms reception in a province by both the province chief and the province senior advisor — usually a U.S. Army senior officer, but after some time the team OIC would begin to be approached to do projects that were not in line with the civic action program objectives. If the team stayed in one location too long they could even find themselves becoming the province public works department. Consequently we made it a practice to relocate teams about every two years. Another continuing problem was to make it clear to the province senior advisor that the Seabee team was not in his chain of command. For certain functions, such as maintaining a portion of a common defensive perimeter the Seabee teams operated together with the Army but by and large the teams operated independently from other U.S. troops.

This was the case whenever we could arrange for it. Our team compounds would be located in an area of the town separate and remote from other U.S. Forces compounds. Every province had a MACV detachment and by '67-'68 numerous other U.S. units were found in practically all provinces. But the Seabee compounds always maintained a degree of separation. When the new teams arrived in Saigon we provided them with their equipment, supplies, as much construction material as we could cumshaw, gave them a map showing their team site, a bundle of piastres (Vietnamese currency) to buy other construction consumables and 30 days to get their team compound built and sent them on their way. Actually we had already made arrangements for temporary living at the site, made contacts with province officials and set up transportation from Saigon to their location. Sometimes it was convoy, other times by cargo flights and in the delta we even used Mike boats to go up the rivers. And once in a while all three methods.

The team at Can Tho was located right on the Hou Giang river, just south of the Mekong. Their compound was like most, a team house, shops, storage, a vehicle parking area and a security perimeter. The team house included a berthing area, office and commo, sick bay, galley and of course a lounge, or bar. Seabee team 0809 was the second team at this site so they took over the previous team's compound. The team bar was rather Spartan — as most all of them were — they had a reefer for cooling beer and soda and a few bottles of booze behind the bar. But the dominant feature of their bar was a big two gallon jar full of green peppers. The jar of

Chapter VI

peppers was another item inherited from the original Can Tho team. I was informed right away that this was the only place in the province where one could get a "really hot pepper." Furthermore the price of a pepper was either free or $1.00. If one became eligible for a free pepper he also was entitled to free drinks at the Seabee team bar for the rest of the night.

The immediate question was: how does one qualify for the free drinks? The team members were quick to spell it out, simply eat one of the peppers without having tears come to your eyes. I had worked in Houston for over four years before the Navy and had eaten my share of hot Mexican food including a goodly supply of peppers. These peppers looked to be just the typical hot jalapenas, about the size of a quarter and round. I had eaten many such peppers as well as other varieties, the really hot ones being red or yellow or pale green and having a long tear drop shape. In any case I figured these jalapenas would not be much of a problem so I promised to have a go at them after work. As soon as I made the commitment all of the team members looked at each other and developed wide "grinners." At that point I should have known that I had been torpedoed.

At the end of the day the Master Chief and I together with the team members retired to the bar. Naturally all 13 team members were there so that they could later bear witness to the fact that they had seen the boss with tears streaming down his face. Actually this was always an all-hands evolution whenever someone tried to qualify for free drinks. But I was ready. Many years earlier I had picked up a trick from my dad having to do with eating peppers. The best method was to pop it in your mouth, close your lips, chew rapidly and swallow. It was important not to open ones mouth during this process.

That's precisely what I did.

Things started out all right. The pepper was really hot, but manageable. After a few quick chews I swallowed the whole thing. At that point a few of the team members began to have a worried look on their faces. But that didn't last long. As soon as the pepper was down I began to feel the heat building up. To begin with my lips became numb. About this same time my innards started to boil. Just a few seconds later the tears began and they kept flowing for some time. By this time the team realized they were in no danger of me drinking free at their bar that night and they all began to laugh. Everybody was laughing, everybody but me, that is. I was still crying up a storm, and my throat was on fire, I suspect steam was coming out of my ears and I could not utter a sound. About this time the team OIC, Lt. J. G. Pete Loberg, handed me a cold beer. I snorkeled through that immediately and didn't taste a thing, but the cold beer sure felt good. I had a second beer right away and began to feel like I might live. I did recover to the point where I could talk again and asked, "What the hell was that?" By this time the team members were roaring like a bunch of tigers. Pete admitted to me that even though the pepper looked a lot like a jalapena it was actually a very hot variety of habanera pepper. It was the same shape, size and color of the jalapenas but that's where the similarities ended. This almost identical appearance gave a lot of folks a false degree of confidence, not only me. I supposed I should have suspected something at the outset. Seabees never give away anything of value for free. But like many others I had to learn the hard way. I did however have some satisfaction when I was told that I went longer than most anyone before the tears began.

About a year later my tour was over and I was headed back to ConUS. The third team was now at the Can Tho site and for almost two years no one had yet managed to earn a free drink at the Seabee bar.

Chapter VII

Blomster Til Mor

THE HEADING, Blomster til Mor, is the title of a famous Norwegian painting by Erik Werenskjold. It shows three young farm girls walking down from the hill, each of them holding a bouquet of wild flowers to take to their mother who is standing in the doorway of the farmhouse. We have had a reproduction of the painting in our house for years. It has long been one of my favorites.

That said, how does that painting become associated with Seabees? I'll get to that. But first, some background.

At the Seabee Center is Gulfport, Miss. in the early '80's the C.O. was Capt. Bob Phenix. He and his wife, Lucy, were perfect for their respective "jobs." At least they were from the standpoint of the battalion skippers and their wives who were home ported there. In addition to being the C.O. of the base Bob was double hatted as the Commander of the 21st Regiment which provided the training and support for all battalions during their home port. His main approach was to do whatever was necessary to support the battalions and at the same time do all he could to keep from levying requirements on us. We all appreciated that. In addition, Lucy was an ideal skipper's wife. She also had "come up through the ranks", so to speak, and was familiar with the trials and tribulations of Seabee wives and the aggravation of long and frequent deployments. She was deeply involved in events for the wives, both officer and enlisted, and encouraged activities and participation by dependents throughout the year.

Her constantly pleasant and smiling countenance made everyone feel welcome and comfortable.

As usual the activities around a Seabee base take on a slightly different tone in early March. Even though the training and deployment preparations continue a lot of effort goes into preparing for the Seabee birthday ball on 5 March every year. There is always a regimental parade, the big Seabee Ball, crowning of the Seabee Queen, battalion picnics — including barbequed alligator in Mississippi — plus other miscellaneous and sundry events, large and small, officially sanctioned and otherwise.

Even so, it was good to get back into the regular routine immediately after the ball. In my case this involved a battalion wardroom meeting of all officers every Thursday while in home port. The meetings were held in the O Club bar after secure. This arrangement provided the opportunity for a cold beer, or two. It also helped to maintain the wardroom identity for all the battalion officers during the home port period. Some of my officers, doctor, dentist, chaplain etc. would work at base clinics and chapels during home port while other officers would be undergoing training apart from the battalion. As much as possible I gathered them all together for our Thursday "training" sessions. These get togethers provided a means for an informal give and take between officers, helped to maintain our battalion identity and enhance the wardroom esprit de corps. Frequently the ops. officer, X.O. or myself would pass the word on certain subjects. In a departure from my enlisted time I never invited the doctor to give a VD lecture. We also used this time as a bona fide training period. I normally tasked one of the junior officers to provide a five to ten minute talk on some subject related to the battalion, CEC post graduate education, construction, military justice, etc. That made the rest of the drinking time justified in my eyes and also let the S-2 training officer mark off a block in his portion of the ops. report.

The wardroom session on the Thursday following the Seabee Ball seemed to be a particularly relaxing time for all of us and I suspect we each had at least one more beer than usual. As you can probably conclude I am building up excuses for what was to come.

As part of the Seabee birthday celebration it is normal to spritz up the base and to install extra decorations and banners here and there. This included the O club bar, which had several floral arrangements. I complemented the bar maid, Mona, on the flowers and she said that was only a small part of them. The dining room was loaded with flower arrangements. I looked in the dining room and sure enough there were flowers everywhere. I asked what was going on and Mona said she thought they

Chapter VII

were left over from the wives club luncheon that Mrs. Phenix had sponsored the day before. When I asked what was going to be done with the flowers Mona said she wasn't sure, nobody had told her anything.

At that point our wardroom session was about to break up. I figured it would be a waste to have the flowers tossed into the dumpster, especially when they could be put to a good use. I told all my married officers, about half of the wardroom, to each take a bouquet home to their wives. After all, the birthday celebration was over, Lucy's luncheon was history, there were apparently no plans for their future use so why let the perfectly good flowers go to waste? Being a romantic soul I thought I would try to pass on some of my talents in that area to my officers. Besides, it wouldn't hurt for them to go home with a peace offering in the way of partial compensation for being at the bar so long. I don't know if it was the response to the skipper's suggestion or their own desire to be nice and romantic, but they cleaned out all of the flowers. They did so well I wasn't left with any to take to my wife.

The next day things were running smoothly — for about 30 minutes. That was when I received a call from Bob Phenix, Commander of the 21st regiment and my boss while we were in home port. Always the gentleman, Bob asked if I perhaps knew anything about flowers at the O club.

At that point I knew, he knew.

I sucked on my teeth like the Japs do when caught doing something wrong or embarrassing, and admitted what I'd done. It seems that Lucy had another luncheon scheduled for the club on Friday and when she prudently made a morning visit to the club to check things out she quickly discovered she had been "deflowered." Well not exactly, but you get the idea.

Bob did not tell me to do anything but he asked if there was any chance I could arrange to get the flowers returned to the O club by 1100. He also said if it could not be done in that time frame not to worry about it as he was sure they could have a nice luncheon without any greenery.

I assured him that one way or the other there would be flowers at the O club by 1100. My first thought was what it was going to cost me to get eight to ten dozen roses delivered ASAP. Randy Williams, my X.O. called in all the married officers and I quickly explained my predicament. Then I told them to saddle up, go home, steal the flowers back from their wives and deliver them immediately to the O club.

In an emergency the Seabee response time can be measured in nanoseconds. In this case that is exactly what happened. All of the flowers were back at the O club well before the luncheon, and even before Lucy made her return trip to the club. Apparently the luncheon came off without a hitch.

But this was not the end of the story, as I still was not out of the woods. Even though it was a poor substitute I went into town after we secured for the day and purchased a dozen yellow roses. I then personally delivered one to each of the wives who had been victims of their "Indian giver" husbands — because of me. They all took it in good graces and the incident become one of our frequent happy hour topics, leading to the question of: is a C.O.'s comment a suggestion or an order? And is it o.k. to disobey an illegal order?

But thank goodness for understanding bosses with a sense of humor. Bob Phenix remained unruffled throughout the episode and to this day when I meet Lucy she breaks out a big smile and asks, "Where are my flowers?"

Chapter VIII

Med Cap

ONE OF THE MAJOR elements of the Seabee team program has always been the medical civic action program (Med CAP) operated by the team corpsman. Naturally his principal mission was to insure the health of the team members and patch us up as need be. But his allowance of medicine and medical supplies was developed such that it provided him with the resources to offer medical care to the locals wherever we happened to be deployed. This was a major element toward achieving what the U.S. ambassador and MACV called the "hearts and minds" effort toward the local populace. In a situation like Viet Nam, where one never really knew which side one of the locals was on — or for how long — the hearts and minds program was crucial.

The corpsman on my Seabee team was R. C. "Doc" Necas HM2. He was a late arrival and did not report aboard until our final week of training. Somehow our battalion seemed to have a continuing problem with all of the staffing that was controlled by BuMed. At one point we deployed without having a medical officer on board. Another time we had two dentists and no doctor. Now we were about to deploy with two Seabee teams, each requiring an independent duty qualified corpsman, but only one was on board. At any rate Doc Necas showed up on San Clemente Island where we were about half way through our field problem. This was the last activity on our training schedule prior to deployment. At this point he had missed out on all team training, language school, SERE training (Marine Corps survival, evasion, resistance and escape school — not what one would call a fun week). While the team members were polite and hospitable enough I could sense some degree of resentment toward the "new guy." In my case I was happy to have a qualified corpsman — finally! But I also had some misgivings about his not having participated in any of our team training. Also Doc was somewhat overweight. Apparently he had been assigned to shore based clinics for too long. This was his first Seabee tour and his specialty was medical equipment repair. I could not see that such a background would be a great benefit to the team over the coming seven months. Still, he was independent duty qualified and a second class petty officer so he met all the essential requirements.

During the remainder of our field problem we experienced no significant medical problems but Doc stood his share of duty watches, helped with the chow preparation, took part in exercise actions and even became part of the crew who went abalone hunting. In addition, he and "Fly" contacted some "partisans" who were actually civil service work crews performing weapons testing on the island. Through this relationship we were able to enjoy some cold beer with our abalone dinner. By the end of the week Doc had established himself with the team members. Even so, he was the subject of friendly kidding by the team while dishing out some of his own. It was apparent that he had now become a full member of the team.

His medical skills were put to use immediately after our arrival in Viet Nam. Our first deployment site was a U.S. Army Special Forces camp at Nam Dong in the mountains south of Hue. A Special Forces "A" team camp had been sited there for several months. They ran operations throughout the area and trained the VNSF (Viet Namese Special Forces). Doc and the Army medic were kept busy patching up the VNSF and the Nung Chinese guard force following their patrols and skirmishes. Later on he did the same with the RF/PF (regional forces/provincial forces) troops. They were nick named the "ruff and puffs" but they were somewhat like a national guard outfit. In any case it was quickly apparent that Doc knew his business quite well. Two months later, after completing our runway and bridge jobs for the Special Forces, we re-deployed to Quang Tri province on the DMZ (Demilitarized Zone). Initially there was not much for Doc to do as the province ran the local hospital/clinic. Consequently he became another builder on the team. Or maybe a laborer. He helped out mixing concrete, by hand most of the time, built forms, drove trucks — but not the end loader. We only had one end loader and I did not want to risk it being down.

Chapter VIII 25

HM2 R. C. "Doc" Necas at the Quang Tri orphanage. Although he received support from the entire Seabee team it was mainly Doc's efforts that resulted in the improvements to the health of the children and also their facilities. BU2 Glenn Dairy is on the right.

Doc did tolerably well as an equipment operator but I did not want to push my luck.

Shortly after we were established in Quang Tri Doc located a local orphanage that held about 30 youngsters ranging from newborn to about 12 to13 years old. He began to make regular visits to the orphanage. The ladies who ran the place were hard pressed to do anything other than feed and clothe the children. Even so they did manage to keep the orphanage and the children quite clean, which was not the norm in Viet Nam at that time. Supposedly the province provided some support but it could not have amounted to much. After his first visit Doc returned to the team house and described just how bleak things were in the orphanage. We contacted the battalion in Okinawa and asked if they could get the families in Port Huenene to help out with children's clothes, infant formula, etc. In no time at all we received several boxes of clothing for babies and youngsters together with cases of canned infant formula and even a good supply of children's toys. The one thing we had overlooked was shoes but we could buy the standard flip-flops in town in all sizes so that problem was quickly solved. Doc and several team members had a field day distributing all the goodies to the kids. The team continued to support the orphanage during the rest of our tour with Doc being the ramrod on the project and keeping us apprised of any special needs we could provide.

During his first visit Doc became acquainted with one particular new born that he nicknamed Pea Wee. In spite of the care by the orphanage ladies and the extra attention by Doc the infant died after a brief time. It was obvious that his death was particularly rough on Doc.

In a short while the team began to work on projects outside of the town proper. We were using a laterite pit west of the town and working on roads throughout the province as well as rural schools, clinics etc. At this point we were given the o.k. by the province chief and the province senior advisor (U.S. Army Major) to hold Med Cap visits. However, they made it clear they could not provide any security. But we never were too antsy about the lack of security as the Med Cap sites would be near to our work sites. At least that's the way it was planned initially. Besides, we soon became aware that Doc was probably treating a number of V.C. at his open house clinics anyhow. But they were at least wise enough not to come to the clinic to have Doc treat bullet wounds. In addition there were always a number of ARVN soldiers and their family members who needed attention. The work the Seabee team was doing was beneficial to most all area residents, including the V.C., so apparently they figured it best not to do anything that might slow or stop that effort.

The Med Caps held close to the work sites near the province capital were always well attended by the locals but the local hospital was also available to them. Doc was probably more proficient than the medical personnel in the hospital — and also free — so he was insured a good turnout. But these nearby Med Cap visits did not do much for expanding the "hearts and minds" program. We needed to get to the folks out in the toolies, who seldom saw any evidence of their government furnishing them any benefits. The goal was to provide a service so that the Vietnamese living in the hinterlands would experience, first hand, some personal benefit courtesy of their government and the U.S. Navy Seabees. Before long Doc began to push out well beyond our work sites. "Bac si", or Doctor in Vietnamese, soon became the most well known and popular Seabee in the province.

Even though his personal safety was pretty much assured by virtue of the medical work, there were places where even Doc admitted the profile on his patients gave him a tight pucker string. When young Vietnamese men of draft age and not in ARVN uniforms showed up in numbers, Doc examined them and provided some medication. But not much. At locations like that we would later talk with the province USAID advisor who consulted his local contacts. He usually confirmed Docs suspicions and supported his decision that we probably should not go back to that particular village. There was no point in querying the MACV folks as they continually maintained the entire province was pacified. Being the northern most province in South Viet Nam and abutting communist North Viet Nam makes one wonder how all the communist troops and supplies made their way south. Admittedly a good portion went via Laos and Cambodia — but not all of it. Consequently we relied heavily on the intelligence recommendation of the USAID rep.

Our team interpreter, Quat, a Nung Chinese, always accompanied Doc on his Med Cap visits. He and Doc were both armed but a carbine and a .45 pistol would not have been much firepower if someone had really wanted to do them in. Early on Quat acted as interpreter, but before long Doc developed a working capability with the language so that he could conduct the medical consultations on his own. Even so, Quat continued to go along to help out as needed. He still served as security and as much as anything he provided a measure of crowd control. This was essential as there were always a large number of potential patients who would appear whenever Doc showed up for sick call, even though the visits were never publicized before hand.

Doc's medications were supplemented by medical supplies from our HQ detachment in Saigon from time to time, but that was really a hit or miss proposition and medicines showed up in whatever quantity happened to be available at the time. Our most valuable help came from Dan Whitfield, the USAID rep in the province. I don't know where Danny got his supplies or how he distributed them, but I suspect he gave a good portion to Doc knowing they would be better used than in the local hospital.

The usual procedure was for Quat and Doc to load a weps (3/4 ton truck) with medical supplies, a field desk in case there was nothing available at the Med Cap site, drinking water, guns and ammo, and head out to the selected location. The chief and I always knew where they were going but we never coordinated with the province or MACV or anybody else ahead of time. Doc generally arrived about mid morning and set up in a clinic, school, or other public building and began seeing patients right away. It was usually mid or late afternoon before he wound up his visit. Frequently he had to secure because he ran out of medications. Other than some rambunctious activity by folks trying to jump the line there were seldom any significant problems. After being in the province long enough to become route qualified Doc concentrated his visits toward the remote areas, in the hills or near the coast, where the residents seldom saw a Doctor or health worker and travel to the province capital was too difficult or too time consuming.

Just like the visits to the orphanage, Doc gained a lot of personal satisfaction from these Med Cap visits. Even so, he also experienced a high degree of frustration from time to time. His biggest bitch usually occurred at the end of his visit when he and Quat were packing up. Patients were still around, usually talking with each other and apparently discussing the medications that Doc had dispensed to them. As might be expected there was quite a variety: big pills, little pills, oblong pills, round pills, some were white while others were blue, tan, yellow, green etc. In any case it generated a situation that Doc never really managed to control. At this point the patients would congregate and compare the medications each of them had received — and then begin to trade pills! Maybe two reds for two whites, a green for a yellow, two small round pills for one big oblong one etc. Apparently their objective was for each of them to end up with at least one of every color and shape. Doc tried to explain how each pill was for a specific malady and their exchanging them was counterproductive — even risky in some cases. His pleas were totally ignored. They would just smile and nod their heads "yes" and keep on swapping pills.

At the end of the day Doc would frequently look at me and ask, "Mr. Olsen, what the hell am I wasting my time for?" It was certainly a valid question and although I sympathized, I had to remind him that even if he might not be making a big improvement in the overall health situation of the Vietnamese people, he was making a hell of a big difference in the local's attitude toward U.S. troops and our ARVN counterparts.

But no matter what I could say just watching the pill swap at the end of the Med Cap visit always caused Doc to just shake his head and mutter to himself as he walked away. Mainly due to his effectiveness Doc was selected to be on another Seabee team during the next deployment. But this time he went out a good bit better prepared. Working together with the team UT (utilitiesman) John "Pea Fly" Peffley, who was from Cincinnati, they arranged for Proctor and Gamble corporation to provide them several thousand motel size bars of soap. The wrappers were printed with the Seabee symbol and the P & G logo. And best of all they were provided free by Proctor and Gamble.

That deployment Doc Necas handed out the bars of soap together with the medications during his Med Cap visits. He maintained they probably did more for the health of the locals than all of his pills. To make things even better he did not have to contend with the locals exchanging the bars of soap.

Chapter IX

Embassy Duty

S OMETIME IN THE EARLY 60's the State Department contacted BuDocks with a request to have the Navy provide trained military personnel to perform maintenance and repair work at U.S. embassies and consulates around the world. The initial concept was for the military personnel to perform low level repair work, i.e. plumbing, electrical, HVAC etc. but they would have to work in all areas of the embassy. Consequently a high level security clearance would be an essential requirement.

The basic criteria for selection of these troops were pretty straight forward and concise. They had to be U.S. citizens, in pay grade E-4 or above (3rd class petty officer), have a spotless disciplinary record, possess or obtain a top secret security clearance and be able to fix anything. Obviously the logical choice was a Seabee.

The program grew over the years and the Seabees in the State Dept. program saw their original tool kit repair tasks expand to include sizeable remodeling and modernization projects as well as to perform inspection work on construction being performed by local contractors. The program still exists with Seabees being assigned around the world.

Embassy duty is considered to be a plum assignment. Being selected for orders to the State Department is quite an achievement. The screening and selection process is rigorous and highly competitive. One of the main benefits of being assigned to the State Department is the fact that those selected can, in most all cases, take their dependents overseas with them. And they usually are able to enjoy a three year tour together. For a Seabee this is almost unbelievable. It is also quite a departure from their usual assignment routine of being ordered from one MCB (Mobile Construction Battalion) to another, year after year.

It did not take long before most all career Seabees began entertaining thoughts about embassy duty. Sometimes it worked out — sometimes it did not. Many of those who were not selected for the State Department program frequently tried to put a good face on it.

When asked by a friend if he had received orders, the Seabees answer was sometimes, "Yep, I'm going to embassy duty", even though that was not the case. The next question was usually where are you going to be assigned? Then the factual answer was forthcoming when the Seabee replied, "Embassy (MCB) THREE, Embassy NINE, Embassy ELEVEN" etc.!

Chapter X

Shower With Mays

BACK IN THE EARLY '60's the DOD policy, before "don't ask, don't tell" came into being, was to discharge any military personnel who were homosexuals. There is no point in generating a discussion over the plusses and minuses of the policy, that's just the way it was. And every now and then such a discharge happened. Not too often in Seabee battalions but they did occur from time to time. And it probably was for the best, both for the unit and for the individual concerned. It was generally not a suitable environment for such a person to remain in a Seabee battalion once their proclivities became known.

But fortunately there was not much need to deal with such a situation nor to be concerned as incidents like that were extremely rare.

The battalion officers and chiefs had been advised to be aware of such behavior and to make it known to the command if it were discovered. To be honest we did not spend much time thinking about activities and behavior of that nature and even less time looking for any indicators. That's why one such "in-your-face" announcement rocked me and my senior chief back on our heels.

Our A Company shops were located in a big Butler building on Okinawa. Even with the equipment doors all wide open it was a hot and humid workplace during the summer months. The company office spaces were on a mezzanine level at one end of the building and furnished with a window rattler air conditioner unit, but I still liked to get out and walk around the shops and yard to get a firsthand look at what was going on. As well as to shoot the breeze with some of my Seabees. Usually my company chief, EOCS "Shot" McCrary or I would make our rounds separately but once in a while we would go together. That was the case this time as we were strolling around the shops talking with some of the mechanics, asking about their work and listening to their bitches etc. One Seabee mechanic who had just reported aboard was working on a grader and he had parts strung all over the deck. He was a young fellow and non-rated (CMCN or E-3) but he obviously knew what he was doing. He was working alone without a petty officer there to supervise him. Even so, the shop supervisor CMC Sam Keeling was nearby and I knew that if Sam had assigned the guy to this task he was for sure up to it. "Shot" and I were asking about various elements of the work and also where the Seabee was from, his family, etc. As usual we also asked what he thought about liberty on Okinawa, chow at the galley and other deployment related subjects. For some reason one of us asked about barracks living conditions. Actually the command was pretty proud of what we had accomplished during our tour as we were able to convince our boss, CBPAC, to allow us to include barracks remodeling in our project list. Granted they were still quonset huts, or as the Seabees frequently described them, half of a big sewer pipe, but they had been totally remodeled. This included new eye-brow windows, resurfaced decks, complete paint out and a reworked and reliable electrical service. The troops still had to use the gang head and shower in an adjacent quonset hut but even so it was quite a step up from the left over WWII quonsets we had inherited.

At any rate the Seabee replied that he thought the barracks were o.k. but the head and showers were not so great. I told him we were working on getting them upgraded but it was not going to happen on our watch. I don't recall the shift in the conversation but the Seabee came up with a comment to the effect that, "The showers probably were not all that bad and besides he really liked taking showers with Mays anyhow!"

No sooner had he made that statement than McCrary and I looked at each other with wide eyes and a "where do we go from here expression." Fortunately the senior chief had the presence of mind to ask why he liked to shower with Mays in particular. Mays was a second class equipment operator in A Company.

The Seabee generated a big sigh of relief for both of us when he said: "It's just like reading the funny papers."

Mays was also one of the few heavily tattooed Seabees in A Co.

Chapter XI

The Washeteria

THE SEABEE TEAM PROGRAM in Viet Nam began in late 1963 with the introduction of four well drilling teams and two Seabee teams — originally called STAT's (Seabee Technical Assistance Teams) — which were assigned to the Army Special Forces. Shortly thereafter the State Dept. became involved and the teams were shifted over to work on "nation building" by concentrating on civic action construction projects under USAID. From the outset CBPAC had established a local area command and support office in-country which was designated CBPAC DET RVN and located in Saigon. By the late 60's the Pacific Seabees were deploying seven Seabee Teams to RVN and the HQ detachment had relocated their offices and quarters to a villa near Tan Son Nhut airport.

In the summer of '67 it was decided by CBPAC and the State Dept. to expand the program up to 15 teams. The first order of business was to work with the USAID staff in Saigon to decide when and where these additional teams would be assigned. Once the deployment dates were established CBPAC could then arrange to ship the team allowances to us. This would have to be done month by month as we did not have much in the way of storage facilities nor any staging area within our compound. In addition, we would have to construct another warehouse building to accommodate our normal resupply stock for teams since we were more than doubling the number of teams. By late '67 the new 40' x 100' warehouse was completed and the additional teams began to arrive in early '68. The first new team arrived in-country just before the Tet offensive by the NVA. But that is another story.

In addition to the preparations for the teams the HQ also had to make some major adjustments. Up to this point the offices were located in spaces within the villa, about two miles from our compound on the far side of Tan Son Nhut airfield. The program expansion also provided for some augmentation of the HQ staff so we would need more berthing and living spaces in the villa. Our total U.S. military staff would go from 10 to 17. This included a personnelman, mechanics, equipment operators, storekeepers and finally a corpsman to manage medical and MedCap supplies. We opened up some space by relocating our offices to the new warehouse building. Our bar area was relocated to the roof top in a new Seabee built space and we covered over a portion of the remaining roof area to be able to show movies in the evening. Previously that had been done in the bar. Most all of the vacated spaces were converted to berthing for the new arrivals. Our dining area was expanded slightly and we enlarged the kitchen/galley by moving all the food storage to a new shed outside the main building.

We figured we were all set. Well, not quite. Like most all small military units in Viet Nam we had hired some of the locals to provide essential personnel support functions for the detachment. Cooks and maids as well as typist/translators were on our payroll plus an older Nung Chinese man we called "papa-san", who handled the laundry for all of us. He had a work area out by the galley and it was a bona fide Chinese laundry. He used large wash tubs to wash and rinse our Seabee utility green uniforms which he dried on a mishmash of clothes lines strung every which way in the available area within the villa walls and away from the vehicle parking. His only acceptance of anything from the 20th century was his use of an electric iron. Everything else was pure hand labor. As a result he seemed to be working all day, every day. And this was to look after the laundry needs of only 10 Seabees. We were due to expand to about 17 in the headquarters staff in the near future. It was obvious papa-san would not be able to keep up. Someone suggested we hire a helper for him but the OIC, LCdr. Seegar Poole had a better idea. Why not get an automatic wash machine and dryer? Obviously that was a logical option but there was a fly in the ointment. We really did not have funds we could legally use for such a purchase. And the appliances as were available in Saigon were particularly pricey. But all the deployed Seabee battalions as well as the 3rd Marine division were

Chapter XI 35

in I Corps and there must be some extra washers and dryers someplace up there.

At that point we turned to EOC DeWeese. The Chief was officially assigned as part of the equipment department of the headquarters. His unofficial, yet actual billet, was that of "cumshaw king." To the uninitiated the term cumshaw is identical to stealing. But to Seabees, sailors and Marines it refers to the reallocation of assets between military units. To the gaining outfit it is a method of obtaining essential material, or items, as rapidly as possible without the rigmarole of red tape and paperwork. To the losing outfit the transaction is usually viewed as grand theft. But in most all cases there is some level of exchange involved even though the compensation, such as it is, might end up in the Chiefs mess, as opposed to being delivered to the units supply yard. The degree of expertise of the two negotiators has a lot to do with who comes out on top. In our case Chief DeWeese was one of the best. While he had been on board he seemed to be able to come up with whatever was needed time after time. It made little difference what the needed items or service happened to be. Construction materials, another generator, food stuff, extra green uniforms for our Nung Chinese guard force, even a guard dog for our compound, the Chief always came through. Also, he was the only member of the headquarters detachment who wore a Rolex wrist watch. But I never really wanted to get into that.

Even so, it would take some special talent and expertise to come up with a washer and dryer. Especially when we realized we did not have much of anything to use for trading stock. However we did have one "ace in the hole." Somehow we had a few commemorative silver coins that had been minted to celebrate the 25th anniversary of the founding of the Seabees earlier that year. They preceded the now popular military coin craze that developed years later but they did not seem to catch on in the 60's. In any case they were all we had and who knows — maybe they would appeal to someone who could do us some good.

The Chief was provided with a supply of Seabee coins and he departed for I Corps (the northern sector of the Republic of Viet Nam) with the departing guidance from LCdr Poole, "Don't even bother to come back if you don't have a washer and dryer."

The Chief was gone for about a week or so before he got back to Saigon but on his return he announced he had the washer and dryer. They were not in evidence so we naturally asked where they were. The Chief said they would be in on the contractor's logistic flight in a few days.

The civilian construction contractor, RMK-BRJ, had their own air cargo fleet which operated throughout View Nam and other supply points in the Orient and they frequently carried items and troops for the Seabees as well.

At that point Seegar hit the ceiling. He told the Chief in no uncertain terms that his instructions were to come back with the washer and dryer, actually to courier them back since they were such precious commodities. He pointed out that even if the RMK-BRJ folks were conscientious about delivering the Chiefs items, the aircraft would make many stops between I Corps and Tan Son Nhut as the contractor was operating throughout the country. And at any of these stops there would be cargo handlers who would recognize the value of the appliances, either for their own use or the exceptionally valuable trading stock, and they were subject to becoming a statistic known as "loss in transit." In short, our washer and dryer were almost certain to end up in either a contractor's camp or some other military location.

About that time Seegar stopped to take a breath and the Chief said something to the effect that the Cdr. should not worry about it as the items would be at the Air Co Fat (Air Cargo Facility Tan Son Nhut, or some similar interpretation) terminal within the week. Seegar was not convinced but what could he do about it at that point. He kept grumbling but eventually he accepted the fact that the only thing to do was to wait. With every passing day he seemed to get more irritated when he thought about the washer and dryer. The Chief kept trying to reassure him that they would show up "any day now" but Seegar was not buying it. But in spite of everything the Chief seemed to be complacent and even rather smug about the entire operation.

Finally we got a call from Air Co Fat operations telling us to come pick up two crates for CBPAC DET RVN. All three of us drove out to the hangar with Seegar grumbling that the crates were probably empty or full of rocks. We saw the crates and the Chief gave them the once over and announced that nothing had been disturbed, they were just as he had packed them. The stencil address read:

        CBPACDETRVN
        Tan Son Nhut
        236K Trung Minh Ky

        MALARIA
        TABLETS

Chapter XI

We got our washer and dryer and a timely reinforcement of the old Navy adage, "Never underestimate a Chief."

Thanks to Capt. A. S. Poole for reminding me of this incident.

Chapter XII

Gamma Globulin

MEMBERS OF THE Navy's Civil Engineer Corps comprise just one of several of the Navy's various and diverse staff corps. (Many of us feel it is the main one.) Other staff corps disciplines include the Supply Corps, Chaplain Corps, Judge Advocate General Corps and of course the Medical Corps. Quite frankly I hold the Medical Corps in the highest regard as they are the folks who patch you up, make you well and often times save your life. But they are a diverse group that includes medical doctors, dentists, nurses and a group titled medical service. And they each have their own individual corps device. It is the medical service corps that is of concern in this story. They are hospital administrators, pharmacists, public health specialists etc. and to a large degree they are made up of former Navy corpsmen. For the most part they are practical, get-the-job-done troops who look at the mission first and the red tape and regulations sometime later. They are also people who you genuinely enjoy being around and having a beer or two with. A word of caution here — they can usually beat the pants off of you in a game of "liars dice." This story deals with an encounter with a MSC officer in Honolulu during the Viet Nam war.

Travel in and out of Viet Nam, or most anywhere in South East Asia or West Pac required a series of inoculations for the various and sundry maladies that might be encountered there. The one I particularly did not care for was the gamma globulin shot. It was not painful but the corpsmen always gave you the injection in the cheek of your butt. Afterwards you walked around all day with the impression that you were carrying a softball in your hip pocket. I don't know what it was supposed to protect you from but it apparently did not do the job as they quit using it sometime later — or switched to another medication. But at that time we had to have the GG shots if we were to travel and most everyone traveled as part of our job. As such we all carried our shot record along with our I.D. card and we were conscientious about keeping it up to date.

During the Viet Nam war most all of the MAC charter flights to Saigon, or anywhere else in the Pacific, made a stop at Honolulu International Airport. Due to the location of Hawaii and the west coast origination of many of the flights they would arrive and depart Honolulu in the middle of the night. This was so commonplace that those of us who traveled frequently referred to MAC as "Midnight Airlift Command."

On one such trip I checked into the MAC passenger desk about 2200 (10:00 p.m.) for a flight to somewhere in West Pac. Air force troops were in charge of the bookings and they all seemed to be sticklers for regulations. Especially so when some airman nothing could tell an officer he could not do something or other. This became even more enjoyable for the airman if the officer was in the Army, Navy or Marine Corps. In this instance I had checked my bag, logged in for the flight and was about to receive my boarding pass. The airman who issued the boarding pass also checked the passengers shot record. Perhaps it was just my imagination but it seemed as if the airman took a special delight as he informed me that he could not give me a boarding pass as my shot record was not up to date. To be honest I did not think that should be the case as I had just had the corpsman poke numerous holes in me about two months earlier in order to bring everything up to date. As it turned out the airman was correct in that my annual gamma globulin shot had expired about a week or so earlier. He did say he would hold my boarding pass until flight time if I could obtain the GG shot somewhere during that period. I knew the CINCPACFLT clinic was closed at that hour but he said some Navy officers had obtained shots at the sub-base clinic, which was supposedly open 24 hours.

I was not very optimistic but I figured I had better do whatever I could to make the flight. But before trying to get transportation over to the sub-base I wanted to make sure I could get the shot. I called the clinic and got a hold of a corpsman who knew about shot records and such and was told that they could give the inoculation but unfortunately they did not have any GG serum on hand and they could not get any before the next day.

At that point it seemed I had exhausted all options so I might as well retrieve my bag, go home and rebook on a later flight. Before heading home I stopped at a bar in the concourse. After all I had been through I told myself I at least deserved a beer. I found a spot at the bar next to a MSC Lieutenant and struck up a conversation with him. He asked how things were going and I replied, "Piss poor."

"What's the trouble?"

I explained that the Air Force wouldn't let me on the place as my papers were not in order, according to them.

"Anything I can do?"

"Not unless you got a gamma globulin shot in your pocket."

"I got something better than that. I got a ball point pen. Give me your shot card."

He wrote the essential information in the appropriate block, signed it with the usual undecipherable signature and dated it and gave it back to me. He also advised me not to go back to the check in desk until shortly before flight time.

I bought his beers, thanked him profusely and got on the plane.

Chapter XIII

English Proficiency

AMERICAN ACCENTS ARE varied and generally easily identified by area. For example, the northeast accent, Texan, Bostonian, southern drawl and even my Kansas twang each have their distinct characteristics. When I was assigned to AFNorth, the northern NATO command in Oslo I was exposed to a slew of Brits. Previously I thought all Brits talked the same — with that funny pronunciation and clipped accents. Not so. I quickly realized that this Brit spoke quite differently from that Brit and so on. I could never distinguish where the speaker might be from but the Brits knew immediately whether the individual was from Cambridge, Liverpool, Plymouth, Birmingham, etc. With Norwegians, Danes and Germans also attached to the HQ it made for some interesting conversations at times.

I recall one meeting with a German Luftwaffe Colonel, the base commander, in the Jagel, Germany O club bar. At the time he was talking with an RAF officer and both were speaking "proper" English. My German host introduced me to the Colonel as Commander Olsen of the American Navy. The Colonel turned to me and said: "Well howdy Commander, welcome to Jagel, I'm right proud to meet ya", spoken in perfect Texan. I soon learned that he had received much of his pilot training in Texas and could have passed himself off as a west Texan easily.

Shortly after reporting aboard AFNorth I was subject to a quick indoctrination regarding the British sensitivity to their proprietary rights of the English language. Lt. Col. Robin Jukes — Hughes, Royal Engineers, came into my office and after a few pleasantries he proceeded to try to rile me with his tongue–in–cheek comment, "Olsen, you're not qualified for this posting. It says very explicitly that for an officer to be given a NATO assignment he must be fluent in the English language — and you're not!" He went on to say "You don't even know the Queen's English." I replied that I did not know it for sure but I had heard that she was. With that Robin shook his head and stomped out, his first attempt to rattle me a complete failure.

But he was correct on one element, there was a requirement that any officer assigned to NATO be fluent in either English or French. And since the French had withdrawn from the military side of NATO several years earlier the French requirement was basically ignored. Naturally all of the officers at the HQ were fluent in English. Some of the Norwegians, Dane and Germans spoke better English than me. But I will say a few of them had a slight accent. And the nationals we dealt with at the various bases were also quite competent in English. Most of them had started learning English early in their elementary schools.

One of the tasks of the infrastructure branch was to conduct maintenance inspections every year to assure that the host nations were properly maintaining the facilities that had been built with NATO funds. Some of these were pretty low key affairs, just the NATO inspectors and the base public works officer. But the Germans took it to the other extreme. It seemed as if every German civil service employee and half of the officer corps assigned to the base would show up for the annual inspection. It was common for the inspection party plus the host nation representatives, civilian and military, to number 40 to 50 people at a German base. (The inspection party totaled three, at most.)

The inspection itself was always a one day event. Consequently it was essential to organize the day's activities and define the schedule at the outset. We started with an organizational meeting early in the morning. As the senior member of the inspection team I was in charge of the day's activities. The inspection party was divided into three groups: C and E (communications and electronics), POL (petroleum, oils & lubricants or more accurately fuel storage, transfer and dispensing) and finally facilities. I began by getting a show of hands from the base personnel as to who would accompany each inspecting officer. The base was always responsible for providing the transportation, which in the case of the Germans was usually a bus and two large vans. I would establish our schedule for lunch and then the time we would reconvene after the inspection. This is

Chapter XIII

what the Germans like to call the "wash-up." Who knows where they picked up the term. Probably from one of my predecessors. This was when the inspectors would meet to review findings and outline our verbal comments to the base personnel. The official written report would not get to them for about two weeks. Following the "wash-up" we would secure and usually retire to the bar.

As mentioned previously there was no requirement for all of the base personnel to be fluent in English but most of them had at least a fair command of the language. Recognizing this limitation I made a point of speaking slowly, enunciating as best I could and using the most basic terms and words. I figured this would enable all those present to understand my remarks. By and large it seemed to work.

At the conclusion of the initial meeting at Nordholtz, a German Naval Air Station in Schleswig — Holstein, a German officer I worked with, Frigatten Kaptein "Charlie" Braun, approached me with a big grin on his face. It was apparent he had something funny to pass on. At our initial meeting I was at one end of a big long table while he was at the opposite end, sitting with several officers from the base. During my remarks another German officer asked FKpt Braun, "His name is Olsen, what country is he from?" It was a logical question. First of all most Navy uniforms the world over are Navy blue with gold striping. The fact that my cuffs had crossed oak leaves rather than stars, if noticed at all, probably added to the confusion. In addition, having the name Olsen I could easily be Norwegian or Danish as well as U.S. or even a Brit or Canadian. In any case it was a logical question. "Charlie" replied immediately that I was an American. The other officer looked back at him rather skeptically and replied, "I don't think so, his English is too poor!"

Sometimes it doesn't pay to try to be helpful.

Chapter XIV

Relieve The Pain

JUST WHEN YOU THINK you have "seen it all" some Seabee is bound to come up with another stunt that causes you to shake your head and wander away mumbling to yourself. In the early '60's at our deployment site of Camp Kinser, Okinawa (later renamed Camp Shield's in honor of the Seabee's first Medal of Honor recipient) such happenings seemed to be an almost daily occurrence. At least it felt that way in Alpha Company of MCB-NINE.

Shortly after reporting to the battalion during home port I was assigned as Alpha Company Commander. In addition to being the largest company in number of troops we were also the orneriest, hardest working, most military and best company in the outfit. (My "A" Co chiefs so indoctrinated me during my first few days on board.) During home port the only characteristic I could truthfully endorse was orneriest. If the old axiom, "work hard — play hard" held true then my company was loaded with hard workers, since I seemed to spend more time at captains mast with my troops than the rest of the Co. Commanders combined. For some perverse reason the "A" Co troops thought this was the way it should be. As the "best" company we always had to do more than the others. It didn't make any difference if the subject was soft ball games, reenlistment rates, project completions, captain's masts or V.D. percentages — Alpha Co had to be at the top of the list.

Compared to our two previous deployment sites, Midway and

Chapter XIV

Adak, Okinawa was a dream come true for the Seabees. A dream come true liberty port with bars, tattoo parlors, pawnshops and girls, girls, girls! What more could any Seabee want? No longer were their liberty hours restricted to sleeping, fishing, walking on the beach and watching Hoot Gibson movies five days in a row. It took the MCB-NINE Seabees about a pair of seconds to adjust to this new and improved situation. By the second day aboard Camp Kinser practically every Seabee on board had made it to Koza, Chibana, Ishikawa and points beyond, and of course sampled the delights of the Island. The sampling involved all the various temptations including the cute Nasans in the area bars. As one might expect a "fringe benefit" so to speak, of all this activity with the Nasans was the anticipated ranking of Alpha Company at the top of the battalion V.D. statistics — again. And sure enough, it came to pass after the first month at our OKI deployment site there was Alpha Co alone and unchallenged — or at least not seriously challenged — at the top of the battalion VD list. Now this listing was not just publicized within the battalion, oh no. We made sure everyone in the Pac Fleet Chain of Command knew about it since these statistics were sent in monthly as part of our Ops report. On one occasion I tried to put this situation in a more favorable light by explaining to the executive officer that Alpha Co was way out ahead of the rest of the battalion when it came to "people-to-people activities" with the locals. As you might expect the X.O. was not impressed.

Even though the company commanders were verbally abused by the X.O. for having unacceptable V.D. rates in our outfits we were never given any information as to the names or the men who made this dubious listing. Such data were private and unavailable even in those days. So there we were — being told to do something to reduce our V.D. rate but not being told who was infected. None of us really knew how to attack the problem other than to hold a "generic prayer meeting" at morning quarters and appeal to the Seabees puritanical interests. Needless to say that never happened. Never the less I was able to learn the names of two of my "A" Co men who were active members of the "scarlet society." This came about accidentally as neither me nor my company chief, EOCS "Shot" McCrary figured we had the spare time — or interest — to chase down our party boys. The first instance happened when our galley chief sent back one of our non-rated men who had been detailed to the galley for mess cooking. As you might expect the chief cook didn't mince words. His memo said something to the effect, "not acceptable — has the clap. Send replacement by 1000 today."

The second instance was a bit more involved and a lot more entertaining. It seems one or my 2nd class EO's had gone to a late sick call for the obvious reason and made a bit of a special request to our Battalion doc — Lt. Jim Mount. "Doc" Mount had served one tour with the 3rd Marine Division on Okinawa before being transferred to MCB-NINE. An Ob-Gyn specialist he liked to say he knew more about VD than any gynecologist alive. Given his Marine Corps & Seabee tours that was probably true. But that's another story.

That evening as all the J.O.'s convened at the ward room bar after secure Doc Mount came over to me with a big grin and asked, Does this guy Valentine work for you? I admitted he was one of my 2nd platoon equipment operators. Doc said he had come in for the afternoon sick call with an advanced case of gonorrhea which he had treated, but he said the Seabee had made a special request which he couldn't accommodate. When I asked what that was Doc chuckled and said, "He wanted me to relieve the pain but leave the swelling."

Chapter XV

Typhoon Condition One

AFTER INNUMERABLE DEPLOYMENTS to Midway and Adak the Seabees of MCB-NINE thought they had won the lottery when they got the word that our next deployment, in early 1963, would be to Okinawa.

Even though the X.O. and the battalion doctor voiced concerns about the potential for a significant rise in our battalion venereal disease rate, practically all of the MCB-NINE Seabees figured that was only minor consideration. And when viewed in the context of prior deployments it might even be one of the highlights of the tour.

As might be expected the deployment began on a high note. The battalion had its' own camp, Camp Kinzer, the projects were challenging and good training, chow was good, liberty was great and we even had decent barracks for a change. Granted they were quonset huts but that was a definite step up from the usual deployment site quarters commonly provided for a deployed battalion. In most cases the station would designate some excess or abandoned buildings as Seabee quarters with the knowledge that we would make improvements while we occupied them. In order to make things a little more habitable that's exactly what transpired. But at Camp Kinzer other battalions had already rehabilitated the quonsets so we just had to move in. Even if they were not the Waldorf-Astoria they seemed so to us.

Being deployed we were not allowed to have private vehicles but that was not a problem. A skochi cab ride into town cost about 35 cents and if need be we could jam up to four Seabees into a tiny Datsun taxi.

Everything about the deployment seemed to be positive but shortly after we arrived in the spring of '63 we did encounter one hiccup. We were soon into the typhoon season. As directed by the U.S. High Commissioner for Okinawa, an Army Lt. General, all activities had a well developed typhoon plan which prescribed various activities to be performed at each stage of the five levels of the typhoon bill.

As best as I can recall the typhoon conditions were somewhat as follows:

Condition 5: No threat, normal weather
Condition 4: Tropical storm in the area
Condition 3: Typhoon in the area
Condition 2: Typhoon expected to hit the island within 24 hours
Condition 1: Typhoon expected to hit the island within 6 hours

These were the general conditions which were applicable to all military installations on the island: Army, Navy, Marine Corps, Air Force — even the Seabees. Each military installation was expected to develop their own individual typhoon bill to address their specific actions for each stage of the warning system and to incorporate appropriate tasks peculiar to their operations. Since the Seabees were always involved in construction the project sites were a primary consideration, in addition to the storm preparations for the camp itself. Previous battalions had developed a list of activities to be accomplished at the various threat conditions. The listings for each stage were quite comprehensive and addressed most all of our unique considerations. For example some of the tasks were as follows:

Condition 5: No action, continue normal activity.
Condition 4: Police job sites and clear or secure loose building materials.
Condition 3: Begin project shut down. Take action to enable projects to survive typhoon winds. Fuel all vehicles. Clear or secure material staged in areas of camp.
Condition 2: Stop project work. Secure job sites. Return equipment and tools to camp. Prepare camp

Chapter XV

facilities for typhoon winds: tie-down shutters, window tapes etc.

Condition 1: All personnel in camp. Living areas stockpiled with water, C-rations. Portable generators distributed and wired in (sick-bay, galley, ops. office, etc). Construction equipment (dump trucks, dozers etc.) staged on each side of large vehicle/ warehouse doors.

As one might expect these actions could account for a significant amount of productive labor hours if they were performed as specified and the storm season happened to be especially active. Never the less the guidance was specific and there was no provision for doing otherwise. Being the "new kids on the block" the first time we experienced a storm warning that altered the condition codes the word came down from the Ops Officer to begin with storm preps. The first storm alert eventually got down to condition 2 before being given the all clear. At that point we used a good many man-hours to move equipment tools and material back to the job sites so more productive labor was lost.

As luck would have it the summer months of 1963 seemed to have more typhoons in the area than normal. And we found ourselves working on storm preps and recovery many times. To be honest, after the first storm prep evolution most everyone in the battalion began to be a little more lax in their execution. But the storm warnings continued and our productive labor hours kept falling month after month. Fortunately we never were hit directly by a typhoon that year but they were all over the Pacific. We did have to send a detachment to NSA Taipei to assist them with recovery efforts later that summer.

Even so, the Ops Officer was none too happy about our severely reduced man hour effort. We also began to observe other military outfits on the island and recognized that while they did not have the same concerns we had i.e. construction projects underway, they did not seem to dedicate as much effort to storm preps as we did, no matter what storm condition was announced.

In some ways this was logical. The Air Force had practically all of their facilities in reinforced concrete structures: barracks, warehouses, hangers etc. Even the Marines had reinforced concrete barracks, courtesy of Seabee construction efforts. But the Seabees were living in quonset huts and all our camp facilities were either quonset huts, elephant quonsets (big ones) or pre-engineered metal buildings. So some extra work on our part was understandable. Even so, the frequency of storm warnings was eating into our productivity.

In order to maintain the work schedule all the company commanders and the project honchos began to let the storm preps slide while we kept working on the projects. As expected, condition 4 was the first category to be ignored. After all a storm warning wasn't much. Before long condition 3 didn't raise an eyebrow with the Seabees and shortly thereafter condition 2 was even ignored.

But the crucial point was condition 1, typhoon to hit within 6 hours. That probably should not be ignored. But in some cases it was! When the island commander set storm condition 1 the Seabees frequently would continue working. Unless the bar girls went home and the skoshi cabs left the streets. When that happened we took it as a bonafide storm warning and headed for the barn as well!

Chapter XVI

The Tonsorial Parlor

FOR THE MOST PART Seabees seem to be closely associated with Marines, and for good reason. To begin with our battalion Gunny Sergeant is the skipper's military advisor and our home port military training is conducted by Marines. In addition, when we deploy we usually find ourselves on the beach with Marines, building support facilities for them as well as the fleet. As a result the Seabee-Marine team is a long standing association ever since it was established in WWII.

On occasion we develop close working relationships with other military outfits. Such was the case during the early stages of the VietNam war. Throughout the period of '62-'64 the Pacific Seabee command deployed Seabee teams in direct support of U.S. Army Special Forces "A" teams. These teams were similar in size and make-up to Seabee teams. The "A" teams were usually headed up by an Army Capt. and a 1st Lt. with 10 experienced NCO's making up the rest of the team. Other than a communications NCO and a medic (Army corpsman) the rest of the enlisted men were mainly weapons specialists. These teams were usually located right in the middle of "bandit country" with Viet Cong (VC) and North Vietnamese Army (NVA) activity being a prerequisite for siting an "A" team camp. At least that's what it seemed like to me at all the Special Forces camps I visited. Their usual missions were to harass VC & NVA units, gather intelligence information and train a Vietnamese Special Forces (VNSF) cadre which was assigned to them.

Several Seabee teams were assigned to the Special Forces to help them develop their camps, build some security features and sometimes improve their logistics capabilities. In my case we were to build two bridges on the only road from the camp to Route 1 and to develop a runway close to the camp that would handle an Army Caribou transport aircraft and ultimately an Air Force C-123 for resupply operations. Up until the airstrip was complete all logistics for the camp was provided by Marine Corps H-34 helicopters out of DaNang. What with the weather, competing requirements for chopper time and the unfriendly neighbors to say that resupply and mail was sporadic was a major understatement.

As you might expect being stuck out in the boonies did not make for the best liberty. Consequently developing some diversions for what little spare time was available sometimes resulted in both ingenious and hilarious activities. Oddly enough haircuts became a big spectator sport — at least for a while. We had some electric clippers, comb, etc. in our pack-up and we had emergency generators around the camp as well as Seabees and soldiers in need of haircuts. What we didn't have was a barber.

No problem.

It was decided that we could just take turns giving haircuts to each other until we discovered someone who possessed heretofore hidden skills as a barber. A more or less logical approach accepted by all concerned. Of course we were all more than gainfully employed during the work day so haircuts had to take place after the project work, return to camp, preparations for the next day and the evening meal. Since it was summer time there was still sunlight at that late hour so all the haircuts took place outside. That way there wasn't much clean-up required. The first one or two haircuts took place with little or no fanfare, each having a different "barber". To no one's great surprise neither "barber" was given any accolades and consequently surrendered the clippers to the next "barber striker" quite willingly.

After observing a couple of these less than satisfactory attempts I decided that I could do considerably better. I had no hair cutting experience either, but crew cuts were in style those days so how difficult could it be? My first customer was EO1 John Beard. John had a crew cut so everything should be easy. After several minutes of clipping and trimming I thought John looked pretty presentable. After a look in the mirror he announced it looked good to him as well.

But the "proof-of-the-pudding" so to speak, was when our team corpsman HM2 Roger "Doc" Necas said he thought it looked fine and sat on the stool for his turn. I felt pretty good about that as none of the other

Chapter XVI

"barbers" had been given a return engagement. By this time I felt pretty confident but since the sunlight was fading I gave Doc a fairly rapid clip. He also wore a crew cut so things went off quickly. I announced I was finished, Doc said thanks and that was that.

However, the next morning as we were eating breakfast the entire team got a look at Doc's new haircut. As I ran the clippers up his head on the sides and back I did a poor job of overlapping the strokes. Consequently Doc had a series of vertical dark hair streaks all around his head. This turned out not to be a popular style or even a new fad, even though I did make such suggestions. I told Doc I would make repairs after work that day but he opted not to let me at him again saying "The only difference between a good haircut and a bad haircut is one day."

In spite of my offer and my one good haircut and my excuse of poor lighting I never got another request for a haircut. Fame is fleeting, I guess.

Later on one of the Nung Chinese guards around the camp took over the barber duties — to everyone's satisfaction. Mine included.

Chapter XVII

Dynamite

NO MATTER WHAT nationality or type of service it seems commonplace for military personnel to adopt animals for themselves or for their unit. There are many pictures of dogs, cats, monkeys etc. together with troops, even in combat areas and in some cases right in the middle of a fire fight. Admittedly the animal usually exhibits the good sense to take cover but still they are right there with their master or handler. There are numerous photos of animals aboard ship and according to some of my submariner friends a good number of even exotic pets have been known to make a cruise aboard a "boomer". I won't go into detail about those sub stories which have been told to me as I'm convinced that submariners lie even more than Seabees.

One of the most well known Seabee incidents of WWII in the Pacific is portrayed by the photo of MM1 Aurelio "Ray" Tassone and a small black dog. Tassone was the Seabee who buried a Jap pill box with his dozer during the invasion of the Treasury Islands. But not being the type to hold a grudge he then adopted the dead Jap soldiers dog.

Since Seabees are normally on the beach with the Marines it makes it much more convenient for them to have a pet. And during Viet-Nam the numerous Seabee battalions, teams, detachments and special units had a good number of pets.

One battalion even had a bear for a pet. And they managed to fly him back to Port Huenene with them at the end of their deployment.

Chapter XVII 55

He was a popular attraction at the Construction Battalion Center for several months before he was eventually transferred to a zoo in the L.A. area.

My Seabee team had a pair of pets. A dog, actually a puppy, and a duck. They were named "Queenie" and "Duck". Not too original but quite accurate. At one point we almost had a snake for a pet. In 1964 my team had redeployed to Quang Tri, the northern most province, and we were given a public building for our team house. We built a shop building out behind where my mechanics could work. One morning I was in the team house working on paperwork and reports while most all the team was out on project sites. All of a sudden CM3 "Johnnie" Johnson runs in and tells me the guards had captured a cobra in our back yard. The guards were local area Vietnamese troops who were a sort of National Guard. Officially called Regional Forces/Popular Forces (RF/PF) we uncharitably referred to them as the "Ruff and Puffs". They lived in a squad tent in our back yard. At any rate they had captured the cobra and when Johnny told me about it he also suggested that we make a pen for it and keep it as a pet. I was not too keen on this idea but I did not make any comment one way or the other. But I was curious to get a look at the cobra, so we went out to the Ruff and Puff tent. With my limited ability to speak Vietnamese and some sign language I eventually got the idea across that we wanted to see the snake. The guard then motioned for us to go with him to their cooking area where he proceeded to take the lid off a pot that was simmering and pointed into it. The cobra had already been butchered and incorporated in the crews evening meal. I never got to see the cobra. On the other hand I never had to contend with making a decision as to whether or not we would have the cobra as a pet (thank goodness) and I never even got to taste the cobra meat.

Three years later I was back in Viet Nam running the Seabee Team program in II, III and IV Corps areas. Shortly before I arrived the HQ Detachment obtained their own guard dog. That may be somewhat of an overstatement since Dynamite had more or less flunked out of guard dog school. One of our Chiefs happened to be visiting the Air Force Security Police K-9 training area one day. I have no idea why he was there in the first place as they would not be expected to have anything we could use in our construction work nor did they have anything worth stealing that we did not already possess. At any rate the Chief quickly made friends with this one year old German shepherd that seemed to be wandering around the place. One of the Air Force trainers commented that he had more or less bilged out of training as he was not aggressive enough and had not exhibited a fierceness they thought was necessary for their work. The Chief said he seemed like a pretty nice dog so he loaded him into the jeep and drove back to the team house compound. That's where he was given the name Dynamite. I have no idea of any reasoning behind the moniker.

Dynamite fit right in immediately. He was automatically the official pet of the HQ detachment personnel as well as our Nung Chinese guard force. And although the Air Force said he was no good as a guard dog we observed just the opposite. We thought he was fantastic. Somehow Dynamite could discern the difference between U.S. and Vietnamese personnel instantaneously. He would growl, bristle, lay down his ears and hold a steady gaze on any Vietnamese who came into the compound. And quite frankly just scare the pea out of most of them. He never did this with the Nung Chinese guards. They seemed to be acceptable to him. It was uncanny how he could distinguish between the Vietnamese and other orientals and westerners. We dealt with one contractor who's wife was half Vietnamese and half French foreign legionnaire. She was quite attractive and visited our compound now and then. But half Vietnamese was enough for Dynamite. When she came for a visit she was given an escort into the house. We also worked with the USAID office in Saigon and folks from their office came to our place from time to time. The U.S. nationals could walk right in. The Vietnamese secretaries got an escort. Obviously the element of wearing a uniform was

He might have been a wash out as an Air Force guard dog but when he "joined" the Seabees as chief of ranch security no outsider dared enter our compound without an escort.

not the discriminating factor as far as Dynamite was concerned. In any case he was a great guard dog as far as we were concerned and as we later collectively agreed — he was probably too smart for the Air Force program.

But Dynamite's most enduring quality was his friendliness to each and every Seabee. In addition to all the detachment personnel we had nearly 200 Seabees in our teams, many of whom traveled into Saigon from time to time. Dynamite was their dog too and he welcomed every one of them. But his friendliness was most pronounced when you returned after an absence of two or three days. With 15 Seabee teams in-country we made it a practice of having the HQ OIC or AOIC visit each team every month. In addition our equipment and supply people and even our corpsman made intermittent visits as well. Most of the visits became a two day trip, even with good military travel connections. These were all fairly routine and did not involve much preparation or coordination. Even so there was some black humor associated with the trips. i.e. when someone would drop you off at the military or Air America terminal they would frequently say: "If you don't come back can I have your stuff?"

On the other hand when you returned from such a trip no one noticed. No one except Dynamite, that is. After being gone for two or more days Dynamite would greet you with his wiggly walk and whine and rub against your leg to be petted. Somehow he know you had been gone and welcomed you home. No one else did. He made you feel like you had been missed and was happy that you were back. It's no wonder that he was every Seabee's favorite pet. LCDR Seegar Poole tried to take him back to the U.S. at the end of his tour but the exit and entry requirements were too unreasonable and time consuming so he had to abandon the idea.

I have no idea what happened to Dynamite when the Detachment HQ was decommissioned in the early '70's. I hope he did not end up in a Vietnamese stew pot.

Chapter XVIII

Such A Deal

NO MATTER WHERE YOU are on the earth water is a concern. In many areas it is a precious commodity. Untold lives have been saved and others lost relative to the availability of water. Likewise fortunes have been made or lost depending on the ownership of water and/or water rights. One of the points always emphasized in survival training is that the human body can rarely survive more than four days without water. Keeping this factor in mind, even Seabees have been known to take advantage of others by virtue of their water production capabilities. But I'm getting ahead of myself.

The availability of water in the middle east registers on everyone in the area. Equally important, however, is the purity or quality of the water. For example the downed aviator floating in an ocean of seawater still has to deal with the problem of potable water for drinking. Potability was likewise a major concern in the jungle and delta areas of Viet Nam. While most every area had plenty of water, and frequently much more than was necessary, it was often polluted and usually carried unwanted parasites.

Fortunately the Navy and Marine Corps had long ago addressed this problem and developed a relatively simple and effective solution. It was called the erdelator. Basically it was a combination pump and filter unit that processed raw water, filtered out the impurities and delivered pure potable drinking water. Sounds like magic. These units

Chapter XVIII

came in various sizes/capacities and the smaller ones were ideal to support our 13 man Seabee teams.

By the mid 60's the Seabee team Civic Action Construction program in Viet Nam had become so successful that the State Department, CINCPAC and COMCBPAC agreed to expand the program from seven to 15 teams. Beginning in January '68 the additional teams began arriving in Saigon. The team deployment sites had been designated and the movement of the team, their equipment and supplies to their particular province in II, III or IV corps took place right away.

The first order of business for the new team was the construction of their compound, complete with living and working spaces, shops, storage areas and a defensive perimeter. Since the team site had to be completely self sufficient they had their own generator as well as a water and sewer system. The team officer-in-charge was given a bundle of piastres (Vietnamese currency) to purchase locally available building materials and the CBPAC Detachment HQ in Saigon also provided as much in the way of building supplies as could be obtained. A good portion of this material was obtained through the tried and true Navy system of cumshaw.

In the Saigon area there were numerous depots of construction supplies just sitting around waiting to be put to use. Unfortunately none of them belonged to the Seabees. OICC-RVN had the largest stockpile followed closely by the Corps of Engineers. But the warehouses and storage yards of Pacific Architects and Engineers were closest to the CBPACDET HQ and they had everything. You could almost see the Seabees drooling as they drove by the PA & E compound. As the public works contractor for MACV, PA & E had all sorts of building materials as well as electrical, plumbing, mechanical and finish items. In short, they were a "one-stop shopping" source for everything we needed to construct a complete Seabee team camp. That was the good news. The bad news was twofold. First, we were not authorized to receive any support from PA & E and secondly, we did not have anything to trade with them as they had it all.

But that was about to change.

Earlier I commented on the erdelator water treatment unit. The filter material on these dandy little units was diatomaceous earth, not something readily available on the local market in Viet-Nam. Consequently this was one of numerous items the Headquarters Detachment had to obtain through the supply system and furnish to the teams on a regular basis. During our preparations for expansion of the Seabee team program by more than 100% we provided CBPAC supply a laundry list of additional requirements. This ranged from bulldozers, backhoes, jeeps and weapons carriers to medical supplies, repair parts, weapons and tools as well as diatomaceous earth and hundreds of other items. As usual the CBPAC supply system responded in a superb manner arranging for most of the larger items (e.g. construction equipment) to arrive shortly before the teams arrived. This was a big help to the HQ Detachment since we were continually low in personnel numbers and moving equipment from the docks to the HQ compound was a big operation. Putting a yeoman or storekeeper or even one of our Nung Chinese security guards on a jeep or weapons carrier was one thing. But loading a dozer onto a low boy or roading a grader through Saigon traffic was something else entirely. In addition, the temporary storage of this extra equipment in our small compound made things more congested than was desirable. The option of using some other unit's storage area was out of the question. In those days a piece of non-allowance equipment in anyone's yard was an open invitation to thievery. Consequently this "just in time" delivery method by CBPAC supply was very much appreciated. Incidentally this method of timely delivery was later adapted and refined by the big three auto manufacturers about 20 years later.

On the other hand, certain items were sent to us all at once in a bulk shipment adequate for all 15 teams. Such was the case with the diatomaceous earth. Usually this would not be a problem since the consumption rate for all 15 teams would run into the range of several hundred pounds a month. I don't recall exactly how much was ordered in preparation for our new teams but I would guess 1200 to 1500 pounds. As it sometimes happens with the supply system, somewhere along the line the unit of issue was changed, and changed drastically. It would have been bad enough to go from pounds to bags but in this case it went from pounds to pallets! And each pallet weighed in excess of 1000 pounds! And here it all came at once. Now we are really into an all hands effort moving hundreds of pallets from the Saigon dock to our compound at Tan Sun Nhut airport. Using our lowboy and highboy trailers and two deuce and a half cargo trucks we moved everything in about six days. Much of the hauling was at night when the traffic was almost non-existent because of curfew regulations. What to do with all these pallets once they were delivered to the compound was another story. LCDR Seegar Poole, who was the OIC of CBPACDET at the time, came up with a brilliant solution. We graded a lane just inside our security fence and stacked the pallets three high all around the compound. We were still subject to being hit by mortar rounds but the danger of small arms fire was a thing of the past. At this point we

Chapter XVIII 61

had the most expensive "sand bag" revetments in Viet Nam but we didn't say too much about that to anyone.

Just about that time the PA & E folks began having trouble obtaining diatomaceous earth for their operations. According to one of their civilian managers their supply system couldn't meet their demands. It did occur to us that our humongous order may have been the cause of their problem but we made it a point not to bring this up in conversations with "outsiders." It became apparent that our little supply problem had evolved into a major advantage for us. With a corner on the diatomaceous earth market in Viet-Nam we were now in the "cat-bird seat" when it came to bartering. One of our Chiefs was designated as the detachment expediter, which was an understood title for the person who did most all of the local procurement. Straight forward local purchases were one thing. Barter and horse trading with other military and military support units was something else again. This was where the time honored Navy tradition of cumshaw was expertly demonstrated by our Seabee Chief. He arranged with the PA & E folks to swap some diatomaceous earth for construction material. As expected, the rate of exchange was exceptionally good — for the Seabees. We would send over a cargo truck with about 50 bags (we never let them see a full pallet) and it would come back with a pallet of plywood, 2 x material, plumbing fixtures, electrical wiring etc. Our only problem at that point was to arrange a shipment of this material to the new team sites all of which were in the Delta. MACV Caribou flights and Air America cargo flights were the preferred means of transport. We were overloading the system considerably for several months. In retrospect it seems that this event was to everyone's advantage. The PA & E folks were pleased that they found an in-country source for their needs, albiet at an obscene exchange rate, and the Seabees got much of the material we needed to help the new teams construct their camps. When I departed in Dec. '68 we hadn't even begun to make a dent in our perimeter revetment.

LCDR Dick Frazier relieved me. I never did think to ask him what all he was able to acquire through the use of our high value trading material.

Chapter XIX

Browning

OUT OF AN 800 man Seabee battalion Tony stopped in front of the wrong man. Wrong for Tony but perfect for me. My battalion, NMCB Seventy Four, was in home port at Gulfport, Mississippi and for admin and training purposes we reported to the 21st NCR. As part of the training regiment Cdr. Tony Corcoran, who was the Chief Staff Officer of the 21st, was making a routine personnel inspection of my battalion. In addition to inspecting the men, their weapons and their 782 gear (the combat paraphernalia worn and carried) Tony also asked individual Seabees pertinent questions pertaining to chain-of-command, Seabee history, specifics on their weapons characteristics, etc. All were perfectly valid questions and admittedly the troops should have been able to reply with the correct answer. That's the theory. In practice it doesn't often work out that way. Usually the most straight forward question is met with a puzzled look, a "What did you say sir?" reply or frequently an "I don't know." And in rare cases the correct answer. But in this case Tony stopped at BU3 Browning and asked a question about his 782 gear. Browning replied immediately and correctly. Tony was stunned. He glanced my way and had an expression on his face that said he could not believe his ears. Not one to give up easily, he asked Browning another question relative to his gear. He received another correct answer right back. Tony continued asking questions, even getting to the functions of certain tabs and pockets. Each time Browning correctly told him their function. To be honest I didn't know half of

Chapter XIX

them myself. Eventually Tony realized he was not about to trip up Browning and he stopped the questions. Other than to ask where he had learned the information on the 782 gear. Browning stated simply, "In boot camp, sir." Tony told me later that Browning was the first Seabee to be able to answer any of his questions regarding the 782 gear. I took the complement without comment but I also avoided mentioning that the boot camp Browning had referred to was Marine Corps boot camp. Before joining the Seabees Browning had served one tour in the Marines.

With his Marine Corps background Browning had considerably more experience with weapons than the average Seabee as well as the tactical aspects of our defensive weapons and military training. Militarily he was knowledgeable and his attitude, and appearance were excellent. He picked up the basics of the builder rate rather quickly and was a good troop leader as well. He seemed to be the ideal petty officer.

As it turned out he did have one flaw in his make-up. He obviously had some latent, but strong, racial prejudice. This element of his make-up went so far as to perhaps cause him to become somewhat unbalanced on the subject, as later events illustrated.

The first incident took place at NAS Sigonella, Sicily where I had a detachment from our main deployment site in Rota, Spain. A short while before the end of our deployment we got word from the Sigonella detachment OIC that one of his men had been attacked in the barracks (we shared barracks space in Sigonella with flight crews and other transients) by a black sailor who cut him using a razor blade. The Seabee who was attacked was Browning and although he did suffer a cut it was a relatively minor nick above his left eyebrow and did not require any stitches. My X.O. gathered as much information as possible over the phone and the detachment OIC confirmed that the local NIS (Naval Investigative Service) office had been informed of the incident and was looking into it. Not surprisingly we were told that Browning had never seen the attacker before and most everyone presumed it must have been a member of an air crew stopping overnight at Sigonella. That was fairly common place in those days. There was no further incident or discovery relative to this event while we were on site and after the NIS reps interviewed Browning they apparently filed the report and promptly forgot about it. Shortly before deploying back to Gulfport the OIC asked for a copy of their report but one was never provided. At this point I began to wonder if the NIS folks even made a report. In any case our deployment was over and the battalion and all detachments returned to Gulfport — the "Redneck Riviera." In effect, we filed it and forgot it as well.

Our next deployment site was Roosevelt Roads, Puerto Rico. Seven months later we found ourselves in the Caribbean in the middle of summer. We had the usual number of detachments out to other Navy and Marine Corps sites and a good work load at every location. In Roosy Roads one of our projects involved rehab work on some of the air stations old barracks. This work was somewhat convoluted as we were given only a few spaces to work on at one time and the rest of the barracks remained occupied. Even so, the work progressed satisfactorily. Browning was assigned to work on this project. About half-way through the deployment we experienced another incident in the barracks involving a black sailor attacking a Seabee with a razor blade. This was in the barracks being renovated and surprise-surprise, the Seabee who was attacked was Browning. According to him the attacker had again used a razor blade above the left eyebrow.

By this time I had a new X.O. and I reviewed Browning's history with him and asked him to look into the matter. It didn't take LCdr Williams long to come up with the conclusion that this was a trumped up incident involving a phantom attacker. Even though Browning continued to maintain his story that he was attacked and he felt that blacks "had it in for him" there was no way to prove or disprove the accusations. Supposedly the attack occurred in the head and there were no witnesses. Even when LCdr Williams pointed out the similarities between the Sigonella and the Roosy Roads attacks; Browning stuck with his story. But the identical elements were pretty amazing. There was no witness to either attack. Browning was attacked by a black sailor who was using a razor blade as a weapon. He had no idea who the attacker was nor why he was the victim. Browning was cut just above his left eyebrow on both occasions. This is a part of the body that a right handed person — such as Browning — could easily manage if he intended to self inflict a blade cut upon himself. The similarities were quite conclusive.

About this time I received a letter from Browning's wife who was upset about the incident and wanted to know what we were doing to protect her husband from this "black marauder".

The X.O. and I beat the subject around for a while and pretty much decided the only person Browning had to be protected from was himself. On the other hand moving him to a different location may be of some value and at least it would give his wife the impression we were sympathetic to her concerns. Although none of the supposed attackers was a member of the battalion we agreed to transfer Browning to our detachment at Gitmo. This happened to be the only

Chapter XIX

detachment we had that did not have a black Seabee as part of the complement.

Following the transfer LCdr Williams continued to follow up on Browning's background. And he came up with a surprising discovery. Although there was nothing that was race related in Browning's Navy personnel jacket it turned out that while he had been in the Marine Corps there was one significant racial confrontation that involved him. At Camp Pendleton, Calif. There was a fight between black and white Marines that involved weapons, knives to be specific. Browning was one of those involved. Apparently there were no significant injuries resulting from the fight and the Marine Corps kept it from becoming too inflammatory but it did make some national newspapers. The participants all supposedly received letters of reprimand and apparently none of them were reenlisted in the Marine Corps. As a result Browning shifted over to the Seabees. All in all the information available regarding the incident was rather inconclusive relative to who did what to whom but it did provide background on a previous incident that involved Browning.

From that point things seemed to stabilize and the work routine kept the troops busy and out of trouble. But it did not last. Late in the deployment we received a call from our OIC in Gitmo advising us of an attack on Browning in the head of the barracks the detachment shared with naval station personnel! And surprise, surprise, it was a black sailor who cut him above the left eyebrow with a razor blade! One would have thought with all the attention given him previously and the questions about the identical elements of the two incidents, that Browning would have come up with a different scenario. At least a razor cut on a different part of his body. On the other hand perhaps he felt his original scheme had been working well so why not stay with it.

Why Browning was pulling these stunts was a mystery to us but the X.O. and I decided a big part of it must be an attempt to foment a racial incident. LCdr Williams put all of his material together and appended our thoughts on the matter and sent the package off to the N.I.S. office in Gitmo. Shortly thereafter they called the X.O. to discuss the matter and verbally admitted they agreed the incident looked like a set-up. They interviewed Browning but apparently their investigation never went beyond that point. Our O.I.C. made several calls to the N.I.S. office but they never provided anything to him, not even a copy of their report. If they made one. Perhaps they had bigger fish to fry.

A short while later we completed our deployment and returned to home port, Gulfport, Miss. Browning's enlistment was over and he was separated from the Navy. He was not given the opportunity to reenlist nor did we encourage him to join the reserves. I have wondered several times how he managed to deal with his problem.

The lack of any action by the folks in the N.I.S. offices, in spite of the apparent wealth of evidence of a scam and the identical situation characteristics is still baffling to me. A false accusation of a crime would seem to merit an investigation just as an actual crime. Perhaps they figured no one was really hurt so forget about it. In any case my earlier high regard the N.I.S. took a big dip — and has never recovered.

But the icing on the cake — so to speak — was when the X.O. received a letter from Browning's wife. After all we had done to defuse the situation as we knew it at the time, and transfer her husband due to the threat to his well being, she complained about the Gitmo deployment per diem rate being lower than the Puerto Rico rate. And, it was costing them money! As the X.O. said to me, "Some days you just can't win."

Chapter XX

Belgian Beer

LOCAL BEERS HAVE BEEN popular for ages and in most cases the locals maintain it is the preferred brew. It's hard to say if that preference is due to loyalty, price or availability — or a combination of all three but in any case it is the preferred beer. Years ago many small towns in America had their own brewery. And in some way we may be returning to that practice with the upsurge of micro breweries in the U.S. which to my biased thinking is a good thing. When I visited China in early '83 I recognized right away that every town had their own local beer. Big bottles, too. Liter size. I confess I could not read any of the lettering on the label but the labels were all different. And the beer was uniformly good. Of course, some of my friends will tell you I never met a beer I didn't like. And that is almost true. This tale is about two of the other category.

Breweries, large and small, have been a long standing tradition and industry throughout Europe. I learned that one of the most dedicated beer brewing and drinking countries is Belgium. I was not all that aware of their dedication to the local brews before a visit in the late '70's. I was making a trip to Brussels to the NATO headquarters together with my Danish colleague, Major Torben Goldberg. Why I brought Torben along I'm not sure. Perhaps it was because of his linguistic capability. He was fluent in about seven or eight languages and could easily manage using another half dozen. Also he knew his way around most cities in Western Europe. But he was not above pulling the rug out from under you on occasion. And when such an event happened he was quick to point out that you were obviously the culprit. To say the least, traveling or working with Torben was always an adventure. It still is.

After settling in to our hotel we made our way to the Grand Place, the famous city square in the center of Brussels. Surrounding the square are numerous fine restaurants and bars as well as other business houses and official offices. Our objective was to find a nice restaurant for dinner. But first, a beer. We had plenty to choose from and since it was late fall we opted for an inside bar as opposed to a sidewalk café. After all it could get rather chilly when the sun went down and we did not want to be bothered with relocating in the midst of our beer drinking.

As soon as we were ensconced in a cozy bar Torben announced that he was going to treat me to one of the most famous of Belgian beers and he gave the order to the waiter — in French. Admittedly I did not understand a word he said. Soon the waiter showed up with a Stella Artois for Torben and a Trapiste, or some such name, beer for me. Since Torben had offered to buy I should have known right away that something was amiss. I tested the Trapiste and being charitable I would say that it was comparable to a poor grade of vinegar. Torben took one look at my grimace and began to roar. He knew beforehand exactly what my response was likely to be and I did not disappoint him.

When his laughter finally subsided he said he knew I would not like that particular beer but he could not resist the opportunity to put one over on me. Which he easily did. But he would make it up. This time he would treat me to a really good Belgian beer. And he again summoned the waiter and gave him the order — again in French. After his little trick I figured I was entitled to a decent beer and soon the waiter showed up with another beer, a dark variety that Torben said was a Guz. Again a big Belgian favorite. I tasted this one and it was worse! To my way of thinking a swallow of GO-90 lube oil would have been much tastier. Naturally Torben was now laughing like a hyena at my discomfort. And the fact that he had zinged we twice made it that much more enjoyable — for him!

He again called the waiter back but this time I talked to him — in English — which I should have done from the outset, and made it plain that I wanted a Stella Artois just like he had served Torben. I had to admit the joke was on me but I did learn something from the incident. i.e. be very careful when dealing with a fun loving Dane.

The crazy part of the entire episode is that Trapist and Guz are actually popular and favorite beers of many Belgians. Somehow I find this hard to

Chapter XX

believe but I guess it is true. Obviously beer tastes vary from country to country and region to region. Even so, I can't imagine anyone in their right mind liking the taste of either one of those two brews.

But there is a sequel to this story. My next job was in JCS (Joint Chiefs of Staff) in the Pentagon. In this assignment I traveled to Europe now and then with OSD (Office of Secretary of Defense) civilians. On one trip to Brussels I pulled this same trick on my OSD traveling companion. He wasn't near as understanding as I had been.

Chapter XXI

When Ya Gonna Make Chief?

ONCE ONE TRAVELS WEST of the Mississippi the knowledge and awareness of the U.S. Navy dissipates rather quickly. The Base Realignment And Closure (BRAC) actions over the past decades have removed nearly all of the Naval Air Stations in the middle of the country so the only significant Navy presence these days consists of recruits and sailors home on leave. And the latter group are seldom in uniform.

The long standing story attributed to many about to retire sailors of throwing an anchor on their shoulder and walking inland until someone asks, "what is that thing?" is not all that farfetched. What with all the lakes and reservoirs built by the Corps of Engineers over the years, midwesterners familiarity with boats and anchors may have made that story obsolete. But the concept of lack of knowledge of things nautical is still quite accurate. Nowhere is that more apparent than in Navy ranks and rates. Somehow seamen, petty officers, chiefs, "jaygees" and Lieutenant Commanders just don't relate to Sergeants and Majors in the mind of most Midwesterners. In fact the only Navy grade that registers any degree of recognition with folks in the prairies is that of the Chief Petty Officer. For the most part they know he is Navy and has a responsible position. Beyond that, their knowledge of what a Chief is, or does, fades pretty rapidly. To some degree the aura and mystique of the Chief is brought about by the CPO's themselves. In most all cases Chiefs are known to be self assured and confident and normally they have no reluctance when it comes to informing the general populace or anyone else within earshot, of their capabilities and exploits. Some of which might even be true. Even so, the knowledge that a Chief Petty Officer is an important member of the U.S. Navy is one aspect of Navy information that seems to register with the population even in the prairie states.

Even though there is a good bit of ignorance of the Navy throughout the midlands there is still a high degree of interest in the Navy by this same population. Back in the days when the Navy shore establishment was divided up geographically by Naval Districts, the Ninth Naval District, which extended from Ohio to Colorado and up to Canada continually, provided more sailors than any other Naval District. And many of the other districts had a much greater population base.

The reason for this significant attraction toward the Navy as opposed to the other services has had numerous theories. For many youngsters from farms, ranches and small towns the lure of going to sea was irresistible. Many of them had never seen an ocean and here was their chance. In addition, it was all paid for and also provided the means to fulfill their draft obligation. This was, of course, prior to the all volunteer force which began in 1974. During that time practically all young men were assured of spending at least two years in one service or the other. Many of us who had seen the Army and Air Force first hand, at bases and posts throughout the midlands decided rather quickly that we did not want to have anything to do with either of those outfits. The lure of the sea and the Navy — as unknown as it was — seemed to be the better alternative. The Marine Corps was also an option but even so it was part of the Navy Department.

One other significant element in the trend toward Navy enlistments had to do with the legal fraternity. More specifically, it had to do with the local justices of the peace in many jurisdictions. This was certainly the case in my home county and this approach was apparently shared by a good many other justices of the peace throughout the state. In the course of their official duties the local judges confronted a number of young men from time to time. Most all of them were of draft age and for the most part the nature of their transgressions were most likely misdemeanors. Even so, some judicial action was usually in order. The justice of the peace in Morris County, Kansas — and ostensibly many others — frequently gave the "accused" the option of joining the Navy right away or accepting an unstated court punishment. In nearly every case the culprit opted for the Navy. The sole option put forth by the court was the Navy. Apparently the judge did not want to risk seeing the offender back in Kansas at some Army or Air Force installation any time soon.

Developments such as these accounted for a considerable number of enlisted sailors but there were also a few individuals who opted for the Navy after graduation from college. As college graduates they were eligible for commissions and through one program or another they emerged as Ensigns. Again the Midwestern public was confounded by Navy officer ranks. For the most part they easily understood where a 2nd Lieutenant ranked in the chain of command but an Ensign? What in the world was that? And even after a few years active duty and a couple of promotions the Navy officer — now wearing "railroad tracks" — was just a Lieutenant. To go back home at that stage was frequently discouraging. A normal farm state conversation might go something like this:

> "Hello Tom, I see you are home for a visit. Aren't you in the Navy now?"
> "Yes Mrs. Smith. I have been on active duty for five years."
> "That's nice, what rank are you now?"
> "I'm a Lieutenant"
> "That's nice. My nephew went into the Air Force last week. He's also a Lieutenant."

One learns quickly that it's not worth the effort to try to explain things. One shipmate from Oklahoma went through an extremely long period of misunderstanding on the part of his parents. Being an only son his dad assumed he would one day return to the ranch and continue to raise white-face cattle. The first indication that such a procedure might be in jeopardy was when the son enrolled in Civil Engineering when he went off to college. Following graduation he went on active duty with a commission in the Civil Engineer Corps. That was a time when the draft required at least a two year active duty period for most all physically qualified males so a couple of years in the Navy did not seem out of the ordinary. But as time passed and promotions accumulated the officer found himself a "two and a half striper" or a Lt. Commander.

The grade of LCDR is probably the most significant for a Navy officer as viewed by the general public. That is mainly due to the unknown associated with that rank. Also there is no similar rank in the Army, Air Force or Marine Corps that has a similar title. Admittedly a LCDR ranks with a Major and wears the same gold oak leaf on his collar but the grade of Lieutenant Commander somehow seems more imposing than that of Major. At least it does with the uninformed general public. And in the

Chapter XXI

case of the officer in question his rancher father even thought he might be doing all right.

For this officer the promotions kept coming. Soon to Commander and thereafter to Captain. Another big disappointment. Of course a Navy Captain ranks with Colonels but most farmers and ranchers equate a Captain with the Army and the company grade officers.

In this case the officer was later promoted to Rear Admiral. When he called home to break the news to his parents he was given only a luke warm reception. His father thought it was fine that he had been promoted again but he seemed not to be too impressed that his son was now a flag officer. As the conversation progressed the officer finally asked his dad if everything was all right. The old rancher finally admitted that he did have some concerns. He said: "All these promotions are probably good, but when are you gonna make Chief?"

There is a follow up to the story as the officer eventually was selected for the position of Commander of the Naval Facilities Engineer Command, the 16th "King Bee" of all U.S. Navy Seabees as well as the <u>Chief</u> of Civil Engineers. He called his dad to inform him of this and pointed out he now was a chief.

The reply from the ranch was profound, "It's about time!"

Chapter XXII

Master Builder Test

SEABEE UNIT DEPLOYMENTS, regardless of the size of the outfit, always have an element of construction involved. And no matter what the mission or where the deployment site may be there always seems to be an element of fun as well. This holds true no matter whether the mission is training, disaster relief, civic action, general construction or combat. In addition, it frequently involves other services and/or units.

Since the Seabees routinely find themselves on the beach with the Marines, the Marines often discover they are the target of the Seabee horseplay. But not all the time. During Viet-Nam the Marine Corps and all the deployed Seabee Battalions were located in I Corps, the northern most provinces of the country. At the same time COMCBPAC, working with the State Department, had deployed 15 Seabee teams to various provinces in II, III and IV Corps. These 13 man teams made up of one CEC Officer, 11 Seabee rates and a Corpsman were normally tasked with civic action construction projects for the province, such as roads, water wells, clinics, schools, bridges etc.

But during the earliest days of the Seabee team program in Viet Nam the Seabee teams were tasked to provide construction support to U.S. Army Special Forces in the building of their "A" team camps. The Special Forces A-teams were comprised of two officers and 10 enlisted men, all experienced NCO's. These A-team sites were always in the middle of "Indian Country", or Viet Cong dominated areas.

Chapter XXII

According to the Special Forces troops that's the way they liked it. This way they did not have to go so far on their search and destroy patrols or their recon patrols. In addition to their combat role the Special Forces Teams were also tasked with training the Vietnamese Special Forces (VNSF) who also occupied the camp. The VNSF were located in what was called the outer perimeter. The A-team, the Seabees and the "inner guard" who were made up of trusted Nung Chinese mercenaries, were located in the inner perimeter which was the main camp. This included the command bunker, communications, armory, sick-bay and living facilities — such as they were. Sometime later the Seabees were assigned only to civic action construction but the connection with the Army Special Forces had been established and Seabee teams often found time to do a few "favors" for their Special Forces buddies.

That was the background when Lt. Pete Ryan took the Seabee team from Mobile Construction Battalion 58 into Chau Doc on the Cambodian border in January 1968. This was right after the Tet offensive and the movement of his team, their equipment and supplies from Saigon to Can Tho and onward to Chau Doc is quite a tale of itself. But that will have to wait. Their team house was a big two story masonry structure built in 1890, according to the inscription over the doors. There was plenty of space for berthing, offices, shops, storage, galley and even a big area used for a combination eating area and bar. Since Chau Doc was right next to the Cambodian border as well as being located on the Mekong River the local area was frequently a "hot" area and enjoyed more than their share of visits by the U.S. Navy's Riverine Force or PBR's. (Patrol Boat Riverine). In addition a Special Forces "A" team was also assigned to the area and had established their camp just a short way out of town.

As might be expected the Seabee house quickly became an after hours meeting place for the U.S. troops in the region. And why not, the chow was good, the beer was cold and the compound had the best defensive perimeter in town. Due to their proximity the off duty Special Forces troops were the most frequent guests. The good natured ribbing and banter between the Seabees and the Special Forces troops was frequently a main topic for discussion. The Special Forces position being that the Seabees were nothing more than janitors while the Seabees claimed that the Special Forces troops were Boy Scout campers operating without adult supervision.

As one might expect nothing was ever resolved during these exchanges except it did help to pass the time. But verbal barbs didn't really accomplish much. So the Seabees decided to add a little something special to the mix. They set up their own version of the master builder test and began to coerce the soldiers into taking the exam. The test itself was pretty straightforward. A stump about 18" in diameter and the same height was brought into the bar and a six inch red circle was painted in the center. The candidate had to hit the red circle with part of an axe blade at least eight out of ten swings of the axe. But he had to do it blindfolded.

In no time all the Seabees became proficient with the axe, even the team Corpsman. And then they began to talk to the soldiers about the test, all the while inferring that passing such a test was highly unlikely for any soldier. Naturally no self respecting Special Forces trooper would let a challenge such as that go unanswered. Once in awhile a soldier would want to know if the Seabees could do it. The answer was always "Hell yes, you want to see one of us prove it?" If the answer was in the affirmative the Seabees would invite the soldier to pick a Seabee — any Seabee — to demonstrate the process. Once the Seabee had been tabbed he would pick up the axe, plant his feet, take the blindfold, swing the axe and practically always hit the red circle dead center. Doing so is not really that much of an accomplishment but the earlier practice helped.

Then it was time for the Special Forces trooper to show his stuff. As one of the Seabees was about to put on the blindfold another one would always holler, "Seabees don't wear shirts we always work bare chested." At that point the Seabee with the blindfold would make the trooper take off his jungle tunic.

In all Navy bars one does not enter covered (wearing a hat) since such a transgression costs the wearer a round of drinks for the entire bar. The Special Forces troops learned this right away and always took off their green berets upon entering and usually put them in a cargo pocket or under a shoulder tab. So now the tunic and the green beret were resting on a chair, and the soldier was ready to begin his builder test.

As one might expect, once you get positioned, striking the same spot with an axe — even while blindfolded — is not really all that challenging. While the soldier is swinging the axe the Seabees are whooping it up with both encouraging words, "Good hit, way to go, etc." As well as "You damn near missed", and "He'll never make it." At the end of the test the Seabees always announce that the soldier passed the test. When he pulls the blindfold off his smile usually fades fast as he sees the axe firmly planted through his green beret just as it had done on nine earlier swings.

Various and sundry reactions usually result with one of the more popular responses from the soldier being, "You rotten bastards" a cold beer and a slap on the back usually put everything right.

Chapter XXII

But the Seabees were careful to initiate only one Special Forces troop at a time. Because they always wanted to bring their buddy back for the builder test the next evening.

Chapter XXIII

The Da Nang Dog

GOING ON LIBERTY WITH a squad of Marines can sometimes be an eye opening experience. One knows at the outset that it for sure will develop into an exciting evening, one way or another, and possibly end up being more of an event than expected. But, of course, that's what was intended from the beginning. The Marine reputation for over the beach landings, fire fights or bar hopping is pretty consistent, i.e. "let it all hang out." One friend who was hosting a cocktail party at his quarters had a coffee table accidentally destroyed by a Marine Major. The Major quickly made it clear to the host that the situation was obviously his fault. He pointed out that he should have known better than to invite a Marine to an indoor party!

But "hitting the beach" (going on liberty) with the Marines is only half of the problem when one realizes that the other half of the liberty party is made up of Seabees. What one group doesn't think of the other has already. And the goal of doing something to top the other guys dumb stunt is always an objective. To make matters worse the situation is compounded when they all collaborate. When that happens the possible outcomes begin to approach infinity.

But I am getting ahead of myself. In the early '60's the Marine Air Wing in Iwakuni, Japan established a helicopter squadron deployment site in Da Nang, RVN. The Vietnamese Air Force had a sizable base at Da Nang and the Marines were given one of their hangars for operations and a collection of one story buildings on the west side of the

Chapter XXIII

base for their use as quarters, offices, dispensary, supply and administrative functions. They were none too luxurious but they did contain all the bare essentials for troop housing and galley facilities. As usual, the Marines were happy to have anything that was a step up from a shelter half.

The squadron operated H-34 helicopters, the workhorse of the Marine rotary wing outfits in those days. Ostensibly, they were there for Sea-Air Rescue in the South China Sea. But they also had a few "collateral duties." The Army Special Forces "C" team was located about a quarter mile away from the Marine compound. They directed the operations of all of their "A" teams in I Corps. These twelve man teams were deployed throughout the Corps and usually located right in the middle of Viet Cong dominated regions. The Special Forces troops seemed to like it that way. It made for a shorter "commute to work." But it also had a few drawbacks, the main one being the fact that the resupply of the "A" teams was frequently a major operation and often had to be scratched at the last minute for various and sundry reasons. Air drops of supplies by Army Caribou or Air Force C-123 Aircraft were the standard means of logistic support but weather, aircraft availability, missing the drop zone etc. all contributed to making the resupply flights pretty much a hit or miss operation. As expected, the Marine chopper flights quickly made the "A" team resupply a more or less routine evolution. They almost developed into a schedule they were so reliable. Weather was still a consideration and common sense and the fact that U.S. Forces in Viet Nam took special pains not to set patterns kept the resupply flights from becoming a regularly scheduled activity. Even so, the resupply of the "A" teams quickly became one of the Marines principal collateral duties and accounted for a good bit of their flight time.

Being close to the Laotian border added another element to the flight planning. Ever so often two Marine choppers would lift off and head west. Later they would return with "passengers" who usually required medical attention. And the passengers normally were quickly flown out of Da Nang. There was not much talk about those flights but they obviously had a high priority at air operations.

So what does all of this have to do with Seabees one might ask? After a few months on site the detachment became aware of a dwindling supply of fresh water. The obvious solution to the problem was to get their own well. While Marines are accomplished at going places and killing people, drilling water wells is not one of their talents. But that's not a problem. After all, if they want something built they need only to call on the

Seabees. We have been doing construction work for the Marines ever since 1942.

Although there were no Seabee units in Viet Nam at that time MCB-NINE was deployed to Okinawa and only a few hours flying time from Da Nang. As soon as the request for well drilling support reached the battalion our OPS Officer, Lt. Jim Bodamer, gave me a call and said to get our well rig ready for airlift and alert a squad of trained well drillers to be ready to deploy to Viet Nam for an indefinite period. The well drilling rig was part of the battalion allowance and already on site at Camp Kinzer on Okinawa. The drill stems, bits, drilling mud etc. were another matter. We had little or no reliable information on the sub surface conditions in that part of the world. That made it difficult to develop a tool and material list for the operation. For some reason everything about the Shu-Fly Detachment seemed to be classified. As a result obtaining background information, or even talking about that particular area was often met with a, "What's your need to know?" question. This was in spite of the fact that every Marine and bar girl on Okinawa knew all about the detachment.

Eventually some geologic information on the area was obtained from the local Army Corps of Engineers office on Okinawa and the essential supplies and equipment were assembled. Picking the well drilling crew was the easy part. EO1 "Pete" Welty was a three hash mark first class, and about to add his fourth. This was not a negative reflection on his abilities. Far from it, as Pete was the ideal squad leader. A Nebraska native who has spent most of his adult years deployed to various Pacific area Seabee work sites, he was an accomplished equipment operator on any type of construction machine that Navy had in its inventory. And he was also an ideal troop leader. The only reason he was not a Chief Petty Officer was that promotions for many ratings, one of them being equipment operator, were essentially "frozen" for many years just prior to the Viet Nam conflict. Pete was what one might consider a classic first class petty officer. Ruggedly built, with a weather beaten face and a voice that could penetrate the roar of a dozer engine and still put the fear of God into any "snuffy" who was not pulling his weight. He was also congenial and a guy you enjoyed sharing beer with. Everything considered, he was just the type of troop leader any officer wanted in his outfit. And to make things easier, his squad had been through well driller training during our last home port period.

In time we managed to overcome all the hurdles and scheduled the movement of the drill rig and troops from Okinawa to Shu-Fly in Da Nang. The drill rig was loaded into an Air Force C-141 with less than an

Chapter XXIII

inch to spare on either side. As my company Chief, "Shot" McCrary said, "It says it's an air liftable rig but it's a good thing they didn't put on two coats of paint." Two of Pete's squad accompanied the drill rig while the rest of the crew traveled to the site on the Marines regular resupply logistic flight. Flight Five went from Iwakuni, Japan to Futema, Okinawa to Cubi Point, P.I. to Da Nang every Tues.

As soon as the crew arrived in Da Nang they sited the drill rig and set up around the clock drilling operations using three crews. The Marines bunked the Seabees in their barracks and the irregular comings and goings of the Seabees didn't seem to be a problem. The situation around the air base and the city was a little tense at that time and earlier the Marine C.O. had restricted the Marines to the base. This also included the Seabees. Their time off duty was spent eating, sleeping, playing poker and playing with the Marines dog.

Shortly after their arrival in Da Nang the Marine "ground pounders" — the "Airdale" Marines in the detachment who were not on flight crews — adopted a scrawny stray dog that was hanging around the area and made him the unofficial squadron pet. With the Marines care and feeding he soon filled out and due to his friendly nature he become everyone's favorite.

Eventually the restriction to the base was lifted by the Marine skipper and the troops who had liberty were soon out the gate and into town. Of course, some of the Marines had the duty and had to remain on board that first day. With the three shift drill schedule some of the Seabees were working and others were due to go on watch so they were also on board. Sitting around and thinking while your buddies are in town drinking and whoring can generate some pretty wild ideas on occasion. And that's just what happened. Actually the first idea was rather innocuous. One of the Marines said he thought it was the dog's birthday and they ought to take him on liberty with them when they went the next day. But at that point rationality went out the window. Very quickly the Seabees and Marines decided they would have to get the dog a present. After all, what's a birthday without a present? And with the organizers being comprised of a dozen or so horny Seabees and Marines the obvious gift would be to get the dog laid. But finding a bitch in heat wouldn't be that easy. So they shifted to plan B. They would take the dog into town to one of the local houses of ill repute and get him a blow job instead. Good thinking, they all agreed. And remember, this was all decided while they were still on base and before they had any booze. Heaven only knows what they might have come up with had they been drinking. The next day about a squad of

Seabees and Marines, and one medium sized dog, went out the gate and into town. They headed straight to their favorite cat-house. Upon arrival they were told they could not bring the dog inside. Apparently some of the more persuasive individuals in the group convinced the madam the dog was their mascot, or some such ploy, and he was eventually allowed inside. Then negotiations began.

Following the French into an area has some definite advantages. For example it was easy to obtain delicious French bread in practically every Vietnamese town, large or small. And nice restaurants were usually easily found with talented chefs, good sauces, soups, desserts and wine. They apparently also introduced the Vietnamese to some kinky sex, as well. When the Shu-Fly crew explained that they were there to celebrate the dogs' birthday with the gift of a little sex the madam wasn't all that surprised. But she assumed the crew wanted one of her girls to give the dog a hand job. The crew quickly clarified their objective and explained it was necessary for some oral sex. Seeing as how it was to be a birthday present nothing less would do. This was a little too much for the madam and she gave them all the bums rush. Seabees, Marines and the dog were soon out the door.

But they weren't giving up.

One of the more "experienced" Marines knew of another brothel on the edge of town that charitably might be described as "not quite so exclusive." As a matter of fact the place was a real shack and the few "working girls" who were there were long past their prime and probably should have left the profession a decade or two earlier. But at least the crew, with dog, were allowed to enter. The madam was quite circumspect but listened to their request. Her initial response was negative, but she didn't throw them out. The more persuasive members of the crew kept talking and after a short while they were discussing the "fee". Even though the dollar to piastre exchange rate was quite good for Americans the Shu-Fly crew had to come up with a sizable number of piastres before they struck a deal. Eventually the pile of piastres was judged adequate and the Shu-Fly crew brought the dog into the room with the old Vietnamese hooker and they lined the room. But the hooker wasn't finished. She made it clear that if the Seabees and Marines wanted to watch it would cost each of them something extra. At that point there was no negotiating on the matter. Each of them made their payment "cash on the barrel head."

And while the Seabees and Marines stood around the perimeter of the room drinking their warm Ba Mui Ba beer and watching, the dog received his birthday present.

Chapter XXIII

Pete Welty later said the dog seemed to develop a special fondness for that particular group from the Shu-Fly crew, and some Seabees even swore that he smiled at them.

Years later the almost exact story was related to me by a civilian construction superintendent who had been an enlisted Marine at Camp Hansen on Okinawa several years earlier. Apparently Marines everywhere have a special soft spot for their favorite dogs.

By the way, we drilled to 403 feet, the last 230 feet being solid granite, and finally were able to develop a 60 gal/minute well. But I doubt that anyone is concerned with that fact.

Chapter XXIV

You're A Yank Ain't Cha?

THE SEABEES HAVE BEEN associated with the Aussies, and Australia in general ever since World War II. There are numerous instances of Pacific area Seabee battalions being sent to Australia for rest and recovery following island invasions. Years later, during the Viet Nam era, Australia was a favorite R & R sites for many U.S. servicemen. While there were several approved R and R sites for the Viet Nam based troops; Hong Kong, Bangkok, Japan, Philippines, Hawaii as well as Australia, it was Australia that was the hands down favorite. Why not? The girls all had round eyes, they spoke English — o.k., with an accent — they were beautiful and friendly. A high percentage of the troops who were eligible for R & R opted for Australia. In fact one Seabee warrant officer told me he had such a great R & R in Sydney that was the only time in his more than 30 years service the idea of going AWOL ever entered his mind. The friendliness of the Aussies was not restricted to the girls. Aussies seem to be one of the most congenial people one can hope to meet. The housewives, man in the street, policemen, store clerks, bartenders etc. are all instant "chums". At least to Americans. And the Australian military are even more so. Perhaps the comrade-in-arms connotation is a factor but the Australian record of being at our side in every modern battle; WWI, WWII, Korea, Viet Nam and even Iraq has earned them a special status with U.S. Troops.

Now if we could just get them to drive on the right side of the road.

Chapter XXIV

But this has to do with a military flight into Australia in early 1967. At that time the U.S. Navy was in the process of constructing two tall VLF (very low frequency) towers on the North West Cape of Australia to facilitate communications with our submarines in the western Pacific and Indian Ocean areas. The program was managed by Pac Div of NavFac in Pearl Harbor with an OICC in Perth, West Australia and a ROICC in Learmonth, on the cape. During the equipment installation stage it became necessary to airlift a large transformer from the U.S. to the site. The Military Airlift Command (MAC) was tasked to carry the transformer from Hawaii on to Australia and I was assigned to be the escort officer. This seemed to be a great collateral duty to me. Two weeks out of the office and a free trip to Australia via Samoa and New Zealand. What's not to like about it?

Due to the size and configuration of the transformer the only Air Force aircraft that could carry it was the C-124. After some back and forth between the Navy and the Air Force a C-124 special lift flight was scheduled and we left Pearl Harbor early the morning of Sunday 8 Jan. '67. The crew consisted of three Air Force Captains; pilot, co-pilot and navigator, two enlisted load masters and one Navy Lieutenant. The first leg was to Pago Pago, American Samoa where we were surprised to see Raymond Burr (TV's Perry Mason) at the same hotel. Our second stop was at Christchurch, New Zealand. We stayed at the NSA Christchurch BOQ which was quite deserted as most all of the troops were on Antarctica, as part of the summer support operations on the "ice." The next leg was to Richmond RAAF base, outside Sydney. There we spent a couple of days sending messages to MAC stating that while delivery to RAAF Richmond is understandably to Australia, the transformers are to go to Northwest Australia, about 3,000 miles further west. Finally they agree to let the crew carry the transformer on to Pierce RAAF base in West Australia. But it was not all wasted time as the flight crew and I got to spend the better part of two days touring Sydney and environs. We left Richmond at 1700 Saturday and arrived at RAAF Pierce early Sunday morning.

As might be expected there was not much activity at the base early on a Sunday and the equipment needed to offload the transformer was nowhere to be had. The station duty officer, a RAAF warrant officer, was apparently counting on a relaxing duty day as he was at the officers club and had already downed a few large bottles of Swan lager. This was well before noon. Even so, he arranged for a truck with a low boy trailer and a heavy duty fork truck to show up and help the loadmasters off load the transformer. This was finally accomplished about mid-day and as it was summer in the southern hemisphere we were a hot and dry crew when the work was done. The warrant officer suggested we stop at the "O" club for a snack and a "libation" before our drive into Perth. Needless to say we all agreed. There was not much to eat at the club but each of us had two or three large bottles of Swan lager. As hot and dry as we were it seemed to evaporate into our innards. Afterwards the warrant officer had arranged for two sedans and drivers to take all of us into Perth, which was about a 30 or 40 mile ride.

The drive from the Pierce RAAF base to downtown Perth goes through a long stretch of fairly desolate country. There are some small towns on the way but nothing of any size until one reaches Perth. About half way to town the Swan lager began to make its presence known and we all prevailed on our drivers to find us a stop with a head. Or as they say in the U.K. and Australia, a "loo." Fortunately we were approaching a small settlement that had a gas station. It was exactly what you might expect in the Midwest in the 30's and 40's. A large old frame house by the side of the road with a drive through in front and two hand operated gas pumps out in front. Naturally the drive was gravel. The driver stopped in front and the six of us piled out and hustled inside as quickly as possible. As mentioned earlier this was on a Sunday and it seems that this "gas station" was also a bar and the social center for the area. As soon as we came through the doors the locals met us with big smiles, warm greetings of "You're a yank, aintcha?" and the last thing we needed, an ice cold bottle of Swan lager with the instructions, "This'll wet your whistle." I have no idea how we managed to do it but I seem to recall we each downed another beer before we made it to the head. And it was not just a one beer stop. We had several, talked to everyone in the bar and even got involved in a couple games of darts before we left the place. Aussie hospitality can't be beat.

Eventually we piled back into the cars and headed again for Perth. Naturally the drivers wanted to know our destination. At this point, I was the source of all knowledge as the OICC folks had told me earlier that they would make hotel reservations. But I was not all together certain of the name of the hotel. All I could remember was that it had something to do with the railroad. Our driver asked, "Could it be the Railway Hotel?" That sounded good to me so I told him that probably was it. As it happened the Railway Hotel was right in the center of Perth. But it was also a quite seedy area, and the hotel itself had seen many better years. The Air Force troops were a little less than pleased when they got a look at the place. And their regard for the U.S. Navy was beginning to drop rapidly. As for myself, after spending years with the Seabees, in Army Special Forces "A" team camps and Marine Corps hooches, I thought it looked o.k. But when I went to the desk to see if we had reservations the clerk looked at me in amazement and said, "Naw mate, we don't make reservations." Not a problem, I thought, so I asked if they had six rooms available. He looked at me, still a little perplexed and asked, "You want the rooms for all night?"

About this time the light was beginning to dawn. The Air Force crew had been talking to the drivers and some of the locals and they quickly realized that we were in the lobby of a local cat house. Needless to say their opinion of the U.S. Navy rose rapidly at this point. As I learned later the construction of the railroads throughout Australia in the early days included the construction of a hotel at every sizeable location. Initially this was for the railroad officials and managers and to some extent the railroad workers. And they were nearly all called the Railway Hotel. As the years went by most of these were supplanted by large and more luxurious hotels and the Railway Hotels deteriorated into second and/or third class hotels and eventually "rent-by-the-hour" facilities catering to the ladies of the night and their customers. Such was the case with the Perth Railway Hotel.

At this point I knew I had to do something, and quickly. I asked the clerk if there was another Rail — something or other — hotel in the area. He said he would check and soon gave me the phone number for the Railton Hotel. He placed a call and sure enough they were holding reservations for six U.S. military.

We got directions to the hotel and piled back into the sedans and drove a few blocks to the Railton. It was a rather new, multi-story Salvation Army Hotel. Not only were there no "chippies" we couldn't even get a beer.

Needless to say I don't think the reputation of the U.S. Navy ever recovered from that revelation. At least not in the eyes of those five Air Force troops.

Chapter XXV

Purple Heart

THE PURPLE HEART MEDAL is considered to be the United States oldest military award. It was originated as an award for merit by George Washington near the end of the Revolutionary War. In 1932 the medal was reauthorized as an award for all U.S. military personnel who were wounded as a result of combat actions.

Like every aspect of military life there are numerous stories associated with the Purple Heart, some true, some probably not so, some humorous and a great many quite somber. One hears tales of individuals who received the award and did not deserve it. There are probably a much greater number of former military personnel who deserved the medal but did not receive it. I can certainly attest to that in the Navy. And there is the issue of justification for the recommendation for award. In my own case I never really knew the criteria, or regulations, that had to be met before an individual was considered eligible for receiving the award. To the best of my knowledge a hard and fast listing of qualification factors did not exist during the early days of Viet Nam ('62-'64). What little guidance I was given was verbal and being a junior officer, jaygee at the time, I simply accepted it and moved on. Viet Nam generated more Purple Heart medals for Seabees than had been awarded in many years. During the period '62-'65 small Seabee well drilling teams were assigned throughout the country to provide water wells for local villages and clinics. This was part of the MACV (Military Assistance Command

Viet Nam) pacification or "hearts and mind" program to generate good will toward the American military personnel who were in-country. We also had a number of Seabee teams (one officer and 12 enlisted) who were originally assigned to work for Army Special Forces. As you might expect these teams and the Army Special Forces A-teams were always located way out in the boon docks. In May '65 full battalions were deployed to Viet-Nam to support the Marines in I Corps, the northern most area of South Viet Nam.

In late '65 the MCB-NINE camp at DaNang east was attacked by VC and NVA forces. Although the attack was repelled the Seabees suffered two KIA and about 65 WIA. Sometime after the attack Lt. Gen. Lew Walt, the commanding general of III MAF in Viet Nam, awarded Purple Hearts to the Seabees. One officer, Lt. Frank Hartman, told me he was expecting to get a Purple Heart for his Purple Heart. He explained it this way. With the Seabees to be decorated in two ranks General Walt and his aide quickly awarded the medals which had a clasp on the ribbon with a metal hook on the back side for a quick temporary attachment to the recipient's blouse, or shirt. In this case it was simply the Seabee green utility shirt. When the general got to Frank he apparently wanted to be sure the medal stayed in place so he hooked it on with some force. The hook went through the shirt all right, and Frank's skivvie shirt and into his chest. After the award ceremony he looked at his sore chest and bloody shirt and announced he needed a Purple Heart for his Purple Heart.

That really was not so far fetched when compared with another story I heard that had to do with the same action. It seems that one Seabee ran for his fighting hole as soon as the attack started and dove into it head first. Unfortunately he was the second person to get the hole and when he came down his face hit the other fellows boot. That was not too serious be he did get a beautiful black eye as a result. And later he was also awarded a Purple Heart.

Among other questionable awards is the issue of the three Purple Hearts received by a 2004 presidential candidate. Lots of media attention and writings on this matter, both pro and con, were abounding that election year. The officer in question had been a member of the river patrol boat squadron on the MeKong River in South Viet Nam. There is no question that such duty was pretty "dicey" every day. Those troops earned their combat pay every day. But in this case the three Purple Heart medals were supposedly awarded for relatively minor injuries. Maybe they were. Maybe they were not. At this date who knows. But what was surprising was the fact that the officer apparently made the recommendation for award of the medals himself! I never knew that was possible. One of the more somber Purple Heart stories has to do with one of my mechanics on Seabee Team 0904 when we were deployed to Viet Nam in 1964. CM3 Dick Bowers or "Bowser" to all the team members, was operating our end loader in a laterite pit just outside Quang Tri city in the most northern province of South Viet Nam. Early on, we had been told not to set patterns or establish regular routines in our work as that made it easy for the V.C. to stage and time an attack. On the other hand this laterite pit was the only one we were authorized to use by the province. Also it was nearby, had good quality laterite and we needed a good bit of it for base material for our roads and some of our construction projects. Even so we were aware of the potential hazard of going to the same site day after day. We had arranged with the province chief to have his troops sweep the road to the pit for mines every day before we went to the pit and the work crew was armed with semi-automatic weapons and loaded magazines as soon as they departed the team house. In time this procedure evolved into a fairly routine practice. The laterite crew drove to the pit as usual on the morning of 19 June '64. As soon as the work crew drove into the pit area they were fired on by the V.C. who had set up an ambush atop the bank where the laterite was being dug out. "Bowser" was hit by three 9mm rounds in his right jaw, chest and right wrist. Led by Chief Corzette the team returned fire and quickly drove the attackers away. "Bowser" was the only one of the crew who was wounded but his injuries were critical. The work crew got him back to the team house right away and our corpsman, "Doc" Necas, stopped the bleeding and cleared his airway immediately. A med evac chopper was requested from Hue and after what seemed an eternity to us it finally arrived. They loaded "Bowser" into the aircraft right away and lifted off the for Army hospital at Nha Trang. A few days later he was transferred to the Oaknoll Navy hospital in Oakland. His recouperation took some time and after we completed our tour in November and returned to Port Hueneme I visited Oaknoll and was there when the C.O. of the hospital presented "Bowser" with his Purple Heart. He suffered the most severe casualty the entire team experienced during our deployment, and received the dubious honor of being the first Seabee to be wounded in Viet Nam.

Even so, he was not the only member of the team to collect some scars in Viet Nam. We experienced a number of minor scrapes, mostly due to mines in or near the roadways. In the area where we were operating in support of the Army Special Forces, the hill country south of Hue, the roadways were more accurately described as trails. Consequently it was

Chapter XXV 91

relatively easy for the V.C. to mine them. We quickly learned how to identify potential areas where mines could easily be planted. Any leaves, grass or tree branches in the roadway, piles of rocks or brush on or near the shoulder, signs of recent digging etc. for the most part should be avoided, if possible. But not always!

One of my team members was driving an Army weapons carrier out to a bridge job when he hit a mine and pretty much totaled the weps. We had "armored" all the trucks, weps and jeeps with one centimeter boiler plate on the floor boards so he did not get any significant injury but "Doc" Necas did patch up a bad cut on his arm. Shortly afterwards I wrote our HQ in Saigon and requested a Purple Heart for him. After some time the word came back from Saigon that the wound would have to be such that treatment by a Doctor was necessary in order to qualify for a Purple Heart award. O.K., they knew the regulations and I obviously did not so that was the end of that.

Later on one of my EO's (equipment operators) was driving a mobile crane we had borrowed from the province when he hit a mine on Route 1, the main highway between Hue and Quang Tri. Again the injury was not life threatening but I thought it justified a Purple Heart so I arranged for him to return to Hue where the MAAG headquarters for I Corps was located. I knew they had a clinic there staffed with Army doctors and I wanted to make sure my guy would have all the justification necessary for award of the medal. Shortly after I sent in the request I received my answer. Yes he was treated by a doctor but it wasn't a Navy doctor. Therefore, no Purple Heart. It seemed I was learning the requirements one step at a time.

Our next mine incident happened during the turn over between my team and our relief, a Seabee team from MCB-FIVE. We were out near the laterite pit and on our return trip we again hit a road mine. We were riding in two weapons carriers and had several members of each team on board. About five or six of us suffered cuts of some degree of severity, mostly minor. In my case I was cut on my big toe, thigh and head, but again none of it severe. Most of the others were about the same. "Doc" Necas cleaned us up and put on some band aids and told us to get out of his sick bay. But the driver of the lead weapons carrier, E03 J.D. Smith was cut pretty deeply on his chin. After his initial treatment Doc suggested we send Smitty down to Da Nang to have a doctor look at him and stitch him up properly. Hue was closer but for some time we had been providing ground support for the Marine H-34 choppers which had staged in an area behind our team house. Ostensibly they were there for any sea-air rescue emergencies off the coast but they seemed to depart toward the west, Laos, every now and then. At any rate they called Da Nang and got the O.K. to scrub their mission and take Smith back to their base. I also knew that the Marine chopper squadron at Da Nang had two flight surgeons, Navy doctors, on board. I was taking no chances this time. The outcome was exactly what I'd hoped for. Smith got stitched up, the Navy doctor signed the entry in his medical record and two months later I was present at a parade in Port Hueneme when Smitty was awarded his Purple Heart.

Later on the qualification requirements seemed to have been slacked off considerably. Even in the Navy. Based on scuttlebutt from others regarding the less rigorous qualification requirements I would guess about half of my team should have been awarded the Purple Heart medal. Still, I am just as happy that I don't have one. I suspect if I were to receive one it would have been for a hole in the head right between the "running lights", and presented posthumously.

One final note regarding Purple Heart medals, again on the humorous side, has to do with an episode involving one of our Seabee team members in Nha Trang in '68. By this time the OIC of the headquarters detachment in Saigon was LCdr. Seegar Poole. I was his AOIC. The information we were given was pretty straightforward and concise. It seems that the team corpsman had visited a local cat house in Nha Trang and somehow ended up with a cut on his pecker. We were never given any more information on the incident and quite frankly we did not want to know any more about it. Even so, Seegar and I could not help but discuss the subject, usually after working hours in the team house bar. As might be expected these discussions were none too serious. But using our beer induced logic we concluded that if the hooker was a V.C. then perhaps the "Doc" had been "wounded during enemy action." Just to clarify things it should be noted that we never did seriously consider awarding a Purple Heart in this case. But since the team was soon due to rotate back to the U.S. we decided some sort of recognition would be appropriate, and we would present it while the team was in Saigon prior to their flight home. Seegar sketched out a design that he called the "purple shaft" and had our shop make up a large tin award. The final product bore a strong resemblance to a phallic symbol. That was the easy part. What took the most time was the award citation. Phrases such as, "while completely surrounded by the enemy" and ". . . penetrating deeply into enemy areas" etc. were incorporated. After some appropriate introductory remarks Seegar made the presentation amid the howls and catcalls by the other team members while the tin medal was accepted by a somewhat red faced team corpsman.

Chapter XXVI

Religious Services

RUNNING THE SEABEE TEAM program in RVN in '68 was for sure a full time job for two of us. After building up to 15 teams scattered around II, III & IV Corps areas our travel requirements became a significant time constraint. In addition we maintained a degree of coordination with the 3rd Brigade in Da Nang, commanded by a CEC Rear Admiral, who was also the senior Seabee officer in RVN. We also dealt with his representative in Saigon, a CEC Captain. Every now and then this coordination could be quite demanding, time wise. We also had official dealings with MACV, OICC RVN, USAID, U.S. Embassy, Saigon & COMNAVFORV which also ate up the calendar.

These were all in addition to our boss, COMCBPAC in Pearl Harbor. But to be honest the folks in CBPAC were probably the least demanding of the lot when it came to levying requirements on us. After all, our program was running quite well and our customers; the embassy, USAID, MACV and the provinces seemed to be satisfied. Therefore CBPAC was tickled pink. Besides their major concern was running the 26 Seabee battalions that were rotating in and out of I Corps in support of the Third Marine Division. In addition they directed the activities of several Maintenance Units deployed throughout the country. The Seabee team program was actually "small potatoes" when compared with CBPAC's overall requirements.

Even so, the folks in Pearl Harbor would come out with an Instruction or Notice every now and then which was addressed to all units, including us. Nearly every one of them were obviously developed with only the battalions in mind but they never the less applied to our tiny operation as well.

One such notice came out in the spring of '68 having to do with religious services. It seemed obvious to us that the Seabee team program should not have been included for two principal reasons. First of all we had no chaplain on the staff and secondly it was extremely doubtful that any of our Seabees would commit a sin! At least that's what we told each other.

But the OIC of the Detachment, LCdr Seegar Poole pointed out that there was a requirement for every unit, including us, to reply to this particular notice. Apparently the Fleet Chaplain wanted to make sure that the heathen Seabees were being given the opportunity to pray. In any case there was nothing for us to do except to answer the mail, so we jointly drafted a rather "tongue-in-cheek" standard Navy three paragraph letter reply to COMCBPAC.

First we listed the facts: we acknowledged the directive to reply and address the religious services program(s) in our unit(s). The second paragraph is the discussion: We pointed out the significant unique characteristics of our specific organization and emphasized that we had neither a chaplain nor an enlisted religious program specialist on board nor did we have a billet for either. We further stated that we recognized the need to provide some degree of religious program support within our limited means and capabilities. The third paragraph is the request or recommendation. In our case we reiterated that we felt the need for some level of religious activity for our teams was foremost in our mind while being mindful of the situational limitations we were forced to deal with throughout the Seabee team operation. After considering all of these objectives and constraints we decided it would be possible to include at least a portion of the standard religious program into our operations. In that regard we requested CBPAC forward to us items number 12 and 13 on the enclosure to the notice.

The enclosure was a listing of those religious program items that should be held by every command to assist in holding services in the field. The listing included such things as a field altar, crucifix, paten, communion crackers etc. And it just so happened that items 12 and 13 were two cases of sacramental wine!

Needless to say we never did receive items 12 and 13. Nor did we even get a formal reply from CBPAC. But Cdr. Frank Newcomb had plenty to say on his next visit.

Chapter XXVII

Anchor Pool

ANCHOR POOLS HAVE BEEN part of Navy tradition probably for as long as we have had ships. For those not familiar with seagoing peculiarities the anchor pool is a gambling scheme based on the time, down to minute and second in some cases, that a ship will drop anchor when it comes into port. Sailors pay a specified amount for each chance and draw or select, a number showing their specific time slot. When the bosun strikes the keeper which lets the anchor fall, the time is recorded in the ships log and that time determines who the official winner will be. Usually the winner receives all the entry money, which provides for a pretty good liberty.

There are all sorts of variations on the anchor pool and probably more to be developed. But I want to tell you about one we had in my Seabee battalion. Admittedly there are no ships in a battalion, hence no anchors. But who said you must have an anchor to have an anchor pool?

Before I get into the specifics I need to provide a little background. In '81 and early '82 my battalion was deployed to Roosevelt Roads, Puerto Rico.

As usual we held quarters after breakfast every day and on Fridays we would have a quick personnel inspection before starting our work day. I would inspect one company, my X.O., ops officer, supply officer, and one other designated officer would each have one of the other companies. We would usually be finished in 12-15 minutes. It seemed to do the trick as Friday uniforms and haircuts were continually acceptable.

Being a tropical deployment site we were authorized to wear the modified Seabee green working uniform. i.e. short sleeve shirts and shorts in lieu of the long sleeve, long pants standard working greens. Wearing this uniform it was easy to spot a new tattoo, and there seemed to be more every Friday. Sometime during our deployment a tattoo artist had set up shop just outside one of the gates to the base. And it was obvious he was doing a land office business. At that time even a small tattoo would cost roughly $30.00 and there were not many small ones. When I would spot a new tattoo I would ask the Seabee when he got it. Usually it was within the week. I was also curious as to the cost so I would ask how much he paid for it. Some troops paid several hundred dollars for the more exotic skin art. I made it a point to ask if their wife or mother knew they had it. In most cases they had not been told. I strongly suggested to the Seabee that he let them know before he showed up at home with it. In any case from my observations the tattoo artist was making a pretty good income. I was amazed at the prices he was charging.

We were discussing the tattoo situation in general terms in the officer's wardroom and all sorts of numbers were being thrown around as to how much money my Seabees had spent on tattoos during the deployment. The "guess-timates" ranged far and wide but there was no way to really know. However, we were about to be relieved by another battalion and return to our home port in Gulfport, Mississippi. Consequently there was soon to be an opportunity to get a fix on the dollar number.

I suggested to the wardroom that we set up our own modified anchor pool with the winning number to be the total dollars spent on tattoos during our Roosy Roads deployment by all of the Seabees who would be on the main body flights home. This excluded those in our four detachment sites as well as the advance party which had already returned to Gulfport to make arrangements for our arrival. That still left close to 500 men in the main body.

I gave one of my Ensigns, Bill Traub, the collateral duty of obtaining and tabulating the tattoo dollars for our anchor pool. Although it took some time it was not a very involved process. Since we were returning home on MAC charter wide body aircraft, provided by commercial airlines, we would have to take care of the manifests, baggage, boarding passes etc. Actually it was a fairly well ordered process. On the day of the flight we set up a series of tables where each Seabee had to log in and provide information relative to the boarding process. All this information

Chapter XXVII

gathering involved using the battalion main body roster. One was to verify weapons serial numbers, another was to check baggage, yet another was to list boarding weight etc. Each man had to get on the scale with his carry on gear so that the MAC folks would have an accurate passenger weight load total. To be honest I was amazed at how much "stuff" the Seabee could cram into their pockets and ditty bags. When a Seabee started the process he was given a boarding number which was his number on the roster and ultimately his boarding pass.

With such a process already in place it was easy to add one more table at the end of the line. This was where Traub and his roster were set up. Bill was pretty efficient. Starting with the boarding number he would ask if man had obtained a tattoo while in Roosy Roads. If the answer was yes he would ask how many. Then he would ask how much the Seabee had paid for those tattoos. He would then record the cost number and say "next." No time for discussion or even an opportunity for the Seabees to ask why he needed the information. Bill told me later he was ready for the troops should anyone ask him a question. He planned to tell them – "You want to get on the plane, don't you"? I'm sure that would have made short work of any queries.

But just because the Seabees did not ask Ensign Traub about the information they were providing did not mean they did not discuss it among themselves. And as usual, their imaginations apparently ran wild. Some opined that getting a tattoo was no longer allowed by Navy Regulations. After all the authorization for sailors to wear beards had been rescinded during our deployment so other similar personnel related actions could easily have been implemented as well. Others thought everyone who got a tattoo at the local artists shop might be in danger of having an infection or a communicable disease. It went rapidly at that point to the conclusion that anybody who had obtained a recent tattoo not only would fail to receive their 96 hour liberty (the usual liberty pass following return from a deployment) but might also be quarantined on base!

There were probably other rumors as well but these were enough to insure a restless flight from Puerto Rico to Mississippi for many Seabees.

Shortly before our arrival in Gulfport, Bill let me know he had tallied up all the numbers. As I recall, the total was somewhat in excess of $12,000.00 and the winner of the "anchor pool" was Lt. Jack Surash. I think he won something like $15.00 I told Bill to get on the aircraft p.a. system and announce the results to the crew, after explaining the reason behind his roster questions. As soon as he made the announcement it seemed as if the entire passenger load let out a gigantic deep breath.

WHEW! Obviously their rumor based fears were figments of their own imagination. And it was good to learn they were not going to be court-martialed or quarantined. And besides, everybody would soon be off on a 96 hour liberty!

Chapter XXVIII

Diego Shore Patrol

*I*N THE VERY EARLY 70's the Seabees made an invasion without Marines. Well all right it was not under fire but it was an invasion never the less. The Seabees went ashore on Diego Garcia, BIOT. (British Indian Ocean Territory)

Following the completion of a joint U.S.-U.K. agreement the Brits allowed the U.S. Navy to construct a communication station on Diego. The island, actually an atoll, is about seven degrees south of the equator directly south of the tip of India. The comm. station was to provide a better means of communication with our submarines in the Indian Ocean. Or so we were told at the time.

Building on a desert island requires some degree of support facilities just to get the supplies, material and troops ashore. Consequently a basic type of reception pier was one of the earliest projects. Of course the Seabees put up their own barracks, galley, shops, storage facilities, etc. right away. But the need for fuel storage tanks quickly became a priority. Working with drums of fuel gets old mighty quick. Diesel and Mogas tanks for vehicles and the comm. station generators were early projects. And now that there were tanks ashore a POL pier with pipelines was essential to transfer the fuel delivered by tankers moored in the lagoon.

Early on it was proposed to construct at least a C-130 capable runway for emergency medical evacuation should it become necessary. After all, they were over 1000 miles from the nearest land and two or three times that to the nearest reliable medical support. And since it was decided to build a runway it might as well be big enough to handle the military cargo jets. Of course they would need jet fuel storage ashore so the tank farm would have to be expanded as would the POL pier and the pipelines. Plus facilities for supporting transit aircraft and crews.

You see where this is going don't you?

The Diego Garcia construction program did not actually "grow like Topsy", but it did grow. Actually it was a very well developed plan. It was however amended many times but it was planned.

My last visit to the island was in early '84. By that time a commercial 747 had made an emergency landing at Diego and shortly thereafter B-52's began operating from the island. If the Air Force was flying from there you know it was pretty well civilized. Later the 3rd Marine Division stationed several of their prepositioned ships in the lagoon and the island provided a valuable support base for actions in Iraq and Afghanistan.

As mentioned earlier the base was not simply an island but actually a U-shaped atoll. On the eastern side were the remnants of an old copra plantation. The western side of the horseshoe contained all the Navy facilities. The road running from one tip to the other was dubbed Route 1.

From its inception until the early '80's all construction was done by Seabees. Contractor personnel were used for some specialized work such as installation of comm equipment but all the brick and mortar work as well as the horizontal construction was put in place by Seabees. For more than 10 years battalions deployed to Diego Garcia, each of them augmented by sizable detachments from every other deployed battalion. This essentially doubled the Seabee numbers on the island.

The fleet also provided some support. A seaplane tender was continually anchored in the lagoon. Their machine shop facilities were a valuable resource for the battalions. They also had another "valuable resource" on board.

"Soft sailors"!

In those days (late '70's) there were no women in battalions and none assigned to the Diego shore station. The first seagoing assignment for women probably was to the tenders as they would normally deploy to an overseas location and stay anchored, or moored, throughout the deployment. Such was the case in Diego.

During my visits to the island in the early '80's it was apparent that most of the female sailors on the tender were not all that attractive. But as they say — beauty is in the eye of the beholder — so that opinion probably changed drastically after a Seabee had been on the island three or four months.

Chapter XXVIII

But that is another story. In any case I have my own theory on how these, less than Miss America, female sailors ended up there. I suspect that the recruiter laid it on the line with some of the homely young girls. Sign up for a fleet rate and I'll get you on a tender. In time you will deploy to Diego Garcia. If you can't find a husband out there you will never find one! That approach seemed to work.

But that's only a theory, of course.

Back to my story.

In the early '80's it was decided by COMCBPAC and PACDIV (Actually the same double hatted CEC Rear Admiral) to start bringing in civilian contractors to accomplish the construction work on Diego. At that point NAVFAC established an OICC office on the island and began awarding construction contracts to civilian contractors. Naturally the Seabee tasking began to diminish. By '83 the only Seabee unit on the island was a detachment from NMCB-62. They were working diligently to finish up most of their projects and to arrange to transfer others, together with project material and equipment, to the new island Public Works Department. And most importantly, to insure that everything was accounted for properly.

I made one of my last visits to Diego in February '83. After my obligatory visit with the island commander — a Brit Royal Navy Commander — I met my Master Chief, Tom Massy, in the Seabee mess for lunch. Tom had just returned from his own visit with Seabees on their project sites. After we were seated he said to me: "Commodore, it's time the Seabees left Diego Garcia."

I replied that a decision to that effect had been made a few months earlier but why did he think so.

He replied: "I just saw two Shore Patrol walking up Route 1 — and they was holding hands!"

I never really asked but I hope one of the SP's was a "soft sailor" from the tender.

Chapter XXIX

Heir Apparent

    VERY NOW AND THEN A person runs across a colleague, or contemporary, who just seems to be head and shoulders above all the rest. In my case I ran into many such individuals, probably largely due to my own limited abilities. But there was one Civil Engineer Corps officer in the '70's and early '80's that many of us acknowledged as being a future Chief of the Bureau, his name was Gene Peltier. His father, also named Gene, had been the Chief of BuDocks during the '55 through '61 time frame.

    That may have had some bearing on Gene attending the Naval Academy where he graduated with a commission in the Civil Engineer Corps. Even the beginning of his active duty was a bit unusual. Unlike most of his academy contemporaries who went into the CEC, Gene met all the physical requirements for a line officer. i.e. he had perfect vision. The normal route for a NPQ (not physically qualified) graduate was a commission in the CEC or Supply Corps. To have a physically qualified graduate go directly into the CEC was unusual in those days. Aside from his physical attributes; i.e. tall, dark and handsome, he was also smart, congenial, pretty laid back and had a dry wit style to his sense of humor. He was an excellent officer and a fun guy to be with. Most everyone thought he was sure to make flag and he probably would have but his untimely death while still a captain abruptly terminated that dream.

    Although we never actually served together we ran across each other several times and we were both in the Pentagon in the late '70's.

Chapter XXIX

Gene was assigned to the office of the Secretary of the Navy — working in government affairs — and I was at JCS. We ran across each other frequently at congressional hearings dealing with military construction. In addition to those duties it was Gene's job to educate the congressional staffers we dealt with on the particular aspects of the Navy and to give them a familiarity with many of the existing Navy facilities. Consequently he traveled with them on their base familiarization junkets. I recall talking with him after one such trip and asking how it went. He said things went fairly well and he thought he had made some significant progress with his Navy indoctrination of a few of the younger staff members. For example he was now fairly confident they could tell the difference between a seaman and a Vice Admiral! They both wear three stripes but there is a whale of a difference between pay grades E-3 and 0-9. I think he told that story just so we could appreciate what a chore it was to educate some of those people.

The chairman of the House subcommittee on military construction once opened his hearing with a long winded soliloquoy reiterating a visit from one of his constituents. He had somehow come up with an impressive figure on the amount of concrete the Department of Defense bought each year. I was not aware we ever ran a tally on that item but I recall it was a big number. At any rate he apparently convinced the congressman that DoD should consider using an alternative which included a proprietary admixture. To be specific, his product. And his big selling point was that by using this substance it would be possible to eliminate sand from the mixture. I almost erupted when Gene leaned over to me and whispered, "This is really going to be big if we have finally found a way to eliminate that expensive sand."

But our most significant collaboration occurred in early '80. Late in 1979 the Iraners had taken over our embassy in Teheran together with a number of hostages. The Russians had moved into Afghanistan and the middle east was pretty much in a turmoil. The powers that be made it known that there was a need for action right away — but not too much action. That guidance evolved into the need to develop a plan for military construction projects throughout the region. The military construction projects were to be sited in "friendly" countries nearby. The countries designated were Egypt, Somalia and Kenya.

Once that word was passed the Joint Chiefs of Staff responded with alacrity — they formed a committee! Maybe that is being a bit facetious but we did convene a joint meeting of all services and unified commands. Each organization sent representatives to D.C. to help develop a list of potential military construction projects for the region. The understood objective of such a program was twofold. First it would be a rapid demonstration of our commitment to the participating countries and secondly the new facilities would augment the host nation's troop support capabilities if the U.S. embarked on military operations in the area.

Although I was only a Commander at the time I was the senior engineer in JCS so the conference became my baby. (Senior engineer — big deal — I had one Air Force Major that worked for me) At any rate when the crowd assembled on a Friday morning I gave them their assignments, by country and spelled out our tasking. We were to develop a listing of construction projects for each country, in general terms; i.e. ammunition storage, fuel storage, general storage, water, hardstands, etc. These were to be bare bones facilities that would satisfy the minimum military requirement necessary to support combat operations. In other words no barracks, gedunks or Air Force officers clubs. Each area group had Army, Navy, Air Force and Marine representatives and I designated a senior officer as chairman of each group.

At this point I reiterated our guidance,

(1) only essential support facilities
(2) establish a rough scope and cost estimate for each line item.
(3) prioritize the listing.
(4) Be done by 1500 — 3 p.m. in civilian time.

This would be essential if the secretaries were to meet the 1600 deadline for the final package.

Looking back on it the officers assembled did a phenomenal job in a very brief time. The rough lists were completed by 1500 and at 1600 when I reconvened the group the typed listings were ready. We passed out the listings to each command representative for their quick review. I thanked everyone for their efforts as well as their quick response and told them the listings would go to the Director of the Joint Staff for further action. Their offices/commands would be kept apprised of any developments.

Up until now there had not been much opportunity for discussion but at this point questions popped up. The first concerns had to do with what U.S. Unified Command and what construction agent (Army Engineers or Naval Facilities Engineering Command) would be responsible for this area. Logical questions since the Department of Defense had never assigned this part of the world to any Unified Command and or made a determination as to the construction agent. I advised everyone that such

Chapter XXIX

determinations were not made by us nor was such a recommendation part of our tasking. We would all have to wait until the "head shed", DOD, announced their preferred designations.

The next question was more germain. Some Army dude stood up and announced that the Army could not agree that the listings were in priority order. I reminded everyone that a prioritized listing was one of our requirements but in order to allay any fears that everything was set in stone I emphasized the fact that it was likely that the listings would be massaged several times before any action was taken. That did not seem to help. The Army rep said again that they could not agree that the list was in priority order.

It was now about 1630, time to secure. Everyone was anxious to get out of the building and head home. I pointed out to everyone that if the listing was not in priority order we all were facing a long weekend right there in the bowels of the Pentagon in those same JCS office spaces. This would involve at least 50 officers, many of whom had traveled thousands of miles to represent their commands at this emergency meeting. I was hoping that peer pressure might influence the Army to back off their objection. But no such statement was forthcoming.

The meeting place was in one of the larger JCS conference rooms dominated by the traditional long green table. About two dozen officers were at the table with an equivalent number on chairs around the perimeter of the room. As the committee chairman I was at one end of the table and somehow Gene was at the opposite end.

At this point Gene spoke up and said, "Just a minute." He took his copy of the report, and with a flourish he opened the cover and began to quickly flip rapidly through the pages. He would stop now and then and mumble comments like, "yeah", "right", "o.k", "seems right", etc. All eyes were upon him as he went through this exercise. In looking back on it now I can fully appreciate what a great performance it was.

After about 30 or 40 seconds he slammed the cover shut and announced, "By God, it is in priority order!"

Nobody said a word. I then excused everyone and promised to send copies of the classified report to their commands. The Army dude kept quiet and we were adjourned.

I could have kissed Gene Peltier.

Chapter XXX

Have A Beer In Bonn

ONE OF THE PRINCIPAL benefits of a NATO assignment is the requirement for a good bit of official travel. The amount of travel varies with the different jobs but it seems most all of them include travel to visit/inspect/observe/attend some function or station. And the travel requirements for the infrastructure (construction) group were among the highest. Not only were we tasked to inspect the site of a proposed project but we also had to make visits during the construction and then annually thereafter. This was to confirm that the host nation was performing the required degree of maintenance and repair of the NATO funded work. And to make the task even more enjoyable the travel included most all of the old cities in Europe. Even though the actual site may have been out in the hinterlands the most efficient travel routing generally would take you through some beautiful old cities. Being assigned to NATO's northern command I traveled around Norway, Denmark, Germany, Netherlands and Belgium. And although they were not in our area of responsibility I managed a few trips to England, France and Austria. All official travel, of course. I can say without reservation if sure beat Adak, Midway, Johnston etc. which constituted some of my earliest official travel.

Most all of our trips included stops or travel through towns whose names became well known during WWII. I recall one incident when I was traveling by train in Germany and with the usual German efficiency the platforms had detailed schedules mounted several places along each platform. Besides the train number they included the name of every stop to the end of the line together with the arrival and departure times. My travel partner was Squadron Leader Sam Parker of the RAF. While we were looking over the schedule Sam remarked, "It looks just like a RAF bombing mission schedule."

In any case the NATO posting did provide the opportunity to see much of Western Europe. One of our many trips included a stop in Bonn, the cold war capitol of Germany. Several of us from the infrastructure branch in AFNORTH were on our way to the annual infrastructure conference at SHAPE but we were making a stop in Bonn to review our portion of the proposed German construction program with our German counterparts before the conference. Actually it was a last minute "compare notes" session to be sure we were all singing the same song. That year we were sending quite a contingent from AFNORTH. The team was headed by our boss, Lt. Col George Barnes, USAF, the branch chief, our programmer a Danish Army Major, Torben Goldberg (later a Brig. Gen.) He was the only non engineer. We kept trying to tell him he was simply our bookkeeper. But instead of accepting the second class status we were trying to thrust on him, he kept insisting he ran the infrastructure branch and further he only kept the rest of us around to tend to the technical details. We had two RAF Squadron Leaders, one for communications and electronics and the other for POL projects. Two British Royal Engineers and another USAF Major, Tom Whitman, from Baltap (the Baltic Approaches HQ on Jutland) rounded out the delegation. A total of eight officers.

Our German hosts had made reservations for all of us in one of the older, but elegant, hotels in the center of town. In fact, it was located right on the platz. Like most European cities the platz is a big open square in the center of town where festivals, concerts, official events, etc. are held throughout the year. Even though it was late September and the tourist season was over there were still some sidewalk cafes around. The weather was nice and sunny and the beer gardens seemed to be doing a good business. I checked into the hotel and spent a few minutes getting settled into the room and happened to look out onto the platz. The ancient buildings and the old world charm were nice to behold but what really caught my attention was the sight of Torben and Tom at a table enjoying a beer. I didn't need any more encouragement. I hustled right down to the open air beer garden. Torben had seen me coming and had already ordered the beer. Actually three beers. The waiter showed up about the same time as I did and Torben informed me it was my turn to pay. I probably grumbled a bit, no Seabee wants to give up without a fight, but I managed to come up with the required number of Deutschmarks.

We sat around talking and enjoying our beer — my first, their third — when we noticed our boss, George, coming out of the hotel. Torben quickly caught the eye of the waiter and ordered four beers. By the time George had walked across to platz to our table, the waiter had delivered the beers and we all informed him it was his turn to pay. George is a pretty easy going guy but he raised the question that maybe we should odd man to see who was to pay. Torben informed him that we had each already paid for one round now it was his turn so there was no need for further discussion. Besides someone else was likely to show up shortly so he would no doubt get his free beer before long. (Looking back at it I now realize that Torben most likely only had to pay for one beer.)

About the time we were draining our steins Terry Tumber, one of the RAF Squadron Leaders showed up on the platz. The same procedure was repeated with him picking up the tab for the five brews. In a way it is hard to believe but the same sequence was followed for the remaining three members of our crew. Lt. Col Mike Hutton, a Brit Royal Engineer, had the "honor" of drinking one beer and paying for eight.

Throughout the episode no one got up to go to the head as we were all afraid we would be on the hook for another round when we returned.

Looking back on it the entire operation went off like clockwork. Eisenhower's invasion of Normandy could have benefitted from such concise scheduling and coordination. On the other hand I have to admit the entire operation obviously came off without a hitch even though there was minimal effort on our part. That just goes to show that no amount of planning and preparation can sometimes out do dumb luck.

Chapter XXXI

Seabee Betty

NO COLLECTION OF SEABEE stories would be complete without some mention of "Seabee Betty". Her name alone brings back memories to literally thousands of Seabees who have deployed to WestPac and other Pacific locations but primarily those deployed to Guam or maybe even those who just transited through the island for the better part of five decades.

Betty, actually Vicenta Chargualaf Peredo, was the unofficial hostess to all Seabees who were ever stationed on Guam. No one seems to know how, or when, she came to that position. It apparently just evolved over a brief time. Betty was frequently described as a gracious, warm hearted person who was friendly to everyone. But she was particularly fond of sailors and had a special affection for Seabees — hence her nickname.

Betty was a unique person in many ways. I'm not sure it was true but she once told me that she was never married. On the other hand she had several children. And she made a point of noting that none of the fathers were Seabees. How that translates into a fondness for Seabees is anybody's guess. Even though she was a single mother she quickly informed listeners that she never received welfare of any sort. She was a super independent person, very resourceful and apparently fairly successful. She also held some strong opinions on most topics and was especially critical of welfare programs.

Betty practiced what she preached. In her words she always

worked, frequently at two jobs. When we became acquainted in the early '80's she held down a responsible management position with an insurance agency as well as being the evening bartender at the NavSta CPO club. She sometimes was called upon to repossess cars which could be a little risky. As such, she always carried a loaded pistol in her purse. On the other hand that characteristic may have developed as a result of her job at the Chiefs club.

In any case she always found time to feed every battalion that deployed to Guam. It is a little hard to comprehend just how she could do that so frequently but she did. This was not just the officers nor even the officers and chiefs, but every last snuffy in the battalion was invited to her home for one of her gigantic fiestas, and made to feel welcome.

Every battalion skipper, and in my case as Commander of the 30th Regiment, asked the same questions. Why is she doing this? What's in it for her? What does she want? The answer became apparent rather quickly — she did not want anything. She liked Seabees and enjoyed being their unofficial hostess on Guam. There was one exception while I was on the island. Betty did ask the battalion skipper for a favor ever so often. Due to the need to prepare for the fiesta and the required clean up, combined with her limited local water supply, Betty would ask if the resident battalion could provide her with a water buffalo full of potable water for the fiesta. Since we were the beneficiaries there was never any question. The Seabees from Alpha Company had a full water buffalo in her driveway the next morning. I suppose some twit reading Navy regs could point out that such an act was not allowed, but fortunately we never did take Navy regs that seriously in the Seabees. After all it really was not to her advantage — it was ours.

One unique aspect of Betty's operation was her collection of official portrait photos of battalion skippers, regimental commanders and officers assigned to ComCBPAC. Her living room walls were literally covered with numerous signed official portraits of Seabee officers. After delivering his portrait to Betty and being shown around her collection Cdr. John Elkins, C.O. of NMCB-62, commented that there was one portrait that was missing. Betty said she didn't think so but John assured her that he was right, but he promised to take care of it. A few weeks later John made another visit to Betty's home and presented her with a signed photo dedicated to Seabee Betty from Ronald Reagan. John's previous tour had been the White House liaison for Chesapeake Division of NavFac, and he still had enough influence and contacts to obtain the signed portrait of the Commander-in-Chief.

Chapter XXXI

The unofficial hostess to all Seabees on Guam. Seabee Betty (Vincenta Chargualaf Peredo) together with RAdm Howard Haynes, COMCBPAC, at the Guam Seabee ball in 1984.

Betty's generosity and hospitality was not totally one way. The Seabees invited her to many events as well. No change of command was ever held without Betty being a member of the official party and having a seat on the dais. And she was always an honored guest at the Guam Seabee balls held every March 5th.

Betty, the Seabees and Guam will be linked together forever. Deployments to Guam will not be the same without her being there. Betty passed away sometime around 2007. But her daughter Debbie has continued to fill the role as unofficial Seabee hostess on the island. Even so, a deployment, or visit, to Guam without being able to spend some time with Seabee Betty will seem incomplete.

The Pacific Seabees will always remember her as our island hostess and patron saint. And she will forever be a part of Seabee history.

Chapter XXXII

What Happened To The Ape?

$\mathcal{A}$ COLLECTION OF SEA STORIES would have to do with sailors, or Marines, one would reasonably conclude. This one is a departure from that theme as it has to do with an Air Force general officer. Actually Brigadier General Palmerton, USAF, started out as a sailor, as he graduated from the Naval Academy. When questioned about it he maintained he took a wrong turn early in his career only because he wanted to fly and he felt the opportunity for a pilot seat was greater in the Air Force. Consequently he took an Air Force commission when he graduated from Annapolis.

General Palmerton and I both arrived at JCS in the J-4 directorate about the same time in the summer of '77. Obviously he was a good bit higher up the chain than me but he was one of my many bosses. Like the other action officers in the Pentagon I often wondered what the flag and general officers did — other than attend meetings and critique our action papers. General "P" did that but he also kept himself well informed on our action issues and he frequently ran interference for us with other parts of the joint staff. He was also very personable and had a good sense of humor. Not surprisingly he was selected for promotion to Major General after a couple of years on board.

Shortly before his departure we held the usual farewell luncheon and the Air Force Colonel who was in charge of the luncheon asked me to deliver a joke or humorous story related to the general as part of the program. Following the meal and the standard plaque presentations etc. it was soon time for my part of the program. The assembled group of Army, Navy, Marine and Air Force officers totaled about 40, most all of us being General Palmerton's staff. I announced I was going to relate an Air Force tale that I had come across during a recent trip to Europe.

I was at the Rhine-Main air base waiting for transportation the following day and naturally decided to spend some of my spare time at the O-Club bar. There were not many officers at the bar but at the far end I noticed an Air Force first lieutenant who had about 15-20 ribbons below his pilots wings. He was an older fellow so my first thought was that he must have been an enlisted pilot. I knew the Navy had used many enlisted pilots during WWII so it seemed likely that he must have had that same back ground. I struck up a conversation with him and commented on his numerous awards and campaign ribbons, several of which I recognized as being WWII campaign ribbons.

This was now in the 70's so something did not compute. I asked if he had been an enlisted pilot and he replied that such was not the case, he had joined the Army Air Corps late in WWII and after flight training he was sent directly to the Pacific. I asked him to pardon my curiosity and forwardness but had he ever been court martialed or reduced in grade? The reply was "oh no" but he did say he was pretty close to a court martial once. At this point my curiosity was over the top and I said, "Well pardon me but you must have nearly 30 years service and you're still a first lieutenant so there's got to be some reason for it." He quickly admitted there was a reason for his lack of promotions. But it was a long story. I told him I had all night.

He was a P-38 pilot flying out of an island in the Pacific near the front lines. They would fly their missions during the daytime and usually return in the evening. After their debrief and chow they would usually hit the sack late at night. Being close to the front they were also subject to attack by the Japs which seemed to occur every night. About midnight or later they would get an alert as a Jap plane was approaching. Normally it was a single aircraft which the U.S. troops nicknamed "bed check Charlie." Radar would track him and at a certain point they would alert the flight crews. When the alert sounded the pilots had to jump into their flight suits and run to the airfield, man their aircraft and start the engines and be ready to launch. When the Jap aircraft was just about to cross the predetermined point where the U.S. planes would launch he would turn back. Even so, the Army pilots had to stay in their aircraft with the engines turning for some time before they could secure. This situation caused quite a problem as the pilots were not getting enough sleep and it was made worse by the fact that they could not even go after the Jap pilot who was causing all the trouble. Such a procedure happened night after night.

After more than a month of this harassment and sleep deprivation growing day by day the lieutenant decided he was going to have to do something drastic to alleviate the situation.

On this particular island it just so happened that there were a number of apes that were identical in size to a small man — or in this case a small fighter pilot. The apes were quite friendly and a number of them had already been adopted as pets by the troops. The lieutenant soon had an ape as his personal pet. He slept under the lieutenant's cot in his tent, fed him regularly and even taught him a few tricks. Then he had a great idea. He would teach the ape how to fly! Well not actually fly but how to start up and shut down the engines on his P-38. Sure enough the ape caught on to these tasks quite easily,

It was not long before the following scenario was taking place regularly. The lieutenant would be in the sack sleeping soundly when the alert sounded waking him and everyone else. The lieutenant would kick the ape sleeping beneath his cot and the ape would get up and put on the lieutenant's flight suit, don the helmet and goggles and run to the aircraft, hop in and start the engines. He would then sit in the cockpit with the props turning until the order was given to secure. At that point the ape would shut down the engines, return to the tent and crawl under the lieutenant's cot and go back to sleep. All the while the lieutenant was getting a good night's rest. This scenario worked just as planned for several weeks. At that point the lieutenant figured he had a good thing going.

But as with most activities, it hit a snag.

One night Charlie did not turn around! As soon as he passed the marker line the order was given to launch.

The next morning the lieutenant was hard pressed to come up with an excuse as to why he did not take part in the air strike. The powers that be were not too understanding but they did not want to hold a court martial and most likely lose a pilot. The end result was that they allowed the lieutenant to stay on active duty but they made it clear he had seen his last promotion. He was now nearing mandatory retirement and still wearing the silver bar of a first lieutenant.

I had to admit it was one hell of a story. And then I began to think of possible after effects and asked: "What happened to the ape?"

The lieutenant replied that he lost track of him shortly after the event but only the other day he had heard that he was somewhere in JCS and had just received his second star!

General Palmerton's laugh was as loud as all the rest and he later told me he would be sure to add this tale to his repertoire of fighter pilot stores.

Chapter XXXIII

Whilst

𝓔VERY NOW AND THEN we are likely to run into a situation, or deal with a problem that you know at the outset is going to ruffle someone's feathers no matter which way it is resolved. You may or may not get your own tit in the wringer in the process but in any case you recognize early on it is not a win-win situation for all concerned. No matter which way you jump it is obvious that somebody or some group is going to be irritated.

In this regard I always envied those "teflon officers" who never seemed to catch any of the blame. To be more accurate I did envy their skill in that regard. I usually did not think that much of them as officers.

Back to the subject.

To take action or state an unpopular position on a matter is pretty much second nature to engineers. If it is the right thing to do, so be it. We normally have solid reasoning for our position so we just let the chips fall where they may. Such occurrences are even more commonplace in staff jobs.

That seemed to be the case when I found myself assigned to a NATO staff in Norway in '75. The infrastructure branch was comprised of five engineering officers and one Danish major who was our programmer. All of us engineers kept telling Torben (who was an artillery officer) that he was our clerk but he continually maintained that he was actually the boss of the branch. The rest of us were all 0-5's, Commanders and Lt. Colonel's but I have to admit the Dane did set the schedule often. But that was not a problem. The problems seemed to be located at SHAPE (Supreme Headquarters Allied Powers, Europe) in Mons, Belgium, and with their international staff. They also had a mix of nationalities and services in their infrastructure office but the major players in Mons were the U.S. officers. This was not surprising as the U.S. was, and still is, the major player, and payer, for NATO's infrastructure construction.

The point where we would sometimes hit a snag was when one of our actions, or endorsements, would be logical from a multinational perspective but they would generate varying degrees of animosity from the U.S. staff officers in Mons. Sometimes we could placate them, sometimes not.

As a result we always asked ourselves: "How will this be received in Mons?" I don't know that such thinking ever changed anything but we did consider that thought. Even so, if we could we would try to deflect the criticism beforehand.

Such was the case in '76 on one of our projects dealing with SAS (Special Ammunition Storage — i.e. nuclear weapons). I don't recall the details but we recognized early on that while our AFNORTH position would most likely be acceptable to the infrastructure folks in Mons there was a high likelihood that the U.S. officers would not be too pleased. The planned changes would impact the current procedures significantly and require some changes. Never the less we had to get our response out right away.

My boss, Lt. Col. George Barnes, USAF, and I put the message draft together more or less saying that AFNORTH supported the subject changes. But before we sent our draft in for typing we talked about possible ramifications from the U.S. officers in Mons. We agreed that they most likely would not be very enthusiastic about our endorsement.

About that time George broke out in a sly little grin and with a twinkle in his eye he said, "But we don't have to take all the blame." I quickly asked what he had in mind and he replied' "We'll make them think the Brits did it." I admitted that was a good idea but I was curious as to how were we going to do it. He said it would be no problem. Somewhere in the text of the message we would simply insert the word "whilst".

Now whilst is a perfectly good English word but almost universally it is used only by Brits. At the time AFNORTH was basically a Brit Army staff, augmented by Canada, Denmark, Germany, Norway and the U.S. The CINC was a Brit Army four star general and the largest percentage of the officers were British.

Chapter XXXIII 119

In any case we figured that any casual observer reading our message would quickly conclude it was prepared by the Brits. At least that was our hope. Anyhow we made the change and that's how the message went out. There was no official reaction from SHAPE.

A short while later we were in Mons and the subject of SAS sites came up. One of the U.S. officers commented to the effect that he could not understand why we even let the Brits have any say on Special Ammunition Storage as they did not control any of the sites. George and I looked at each other and smiled.

Success!

Chapter XXXIV

Good Soup

*D*URING THE PEAK YEARS OF Viet-Nam, '67-'69, all of the Seabees in-country fell under the command of the 3rd Brigade. The brigade commander at that time was RAdm Jim Bartlett. The 3rd Brigade headquarters was in DaNang in an old rubble masonry and plaster building known as "The White Elephant." Sometime later they relocated to a new headquarters building near China Beach but still in the DaNang area. Practically all of Admiral Bartlett's command, two Seabee regiments and up to a dozen battalions were assigned to I Corps (Eye Corps as the troops called it) which included the four northern provinces of South Viet Nam. That was understandable considering that all of the Marines in Viet Nam were also assigned throughout I Corps.

The Admirals Seabee command also included a Maintenance Unit at Cam Ranh Bay and the Seabee Team headquarters in Saigon, plus the in-country Seabee teams. The Seabee Team headquarters was actually located on Tan Son Nhut airport property, Saigon International Airport, and for several years the busiest airport in the world. The teams themselves were scattered throughout II, III & IV Corps and were involved with Civic Action Construction projects for the villages and provinces. The 3rd Brigade also maintained a liaison office in Saigon, run by a CEC Captain, to provide a point of contact between the Seabee construction effort and the larger construction program being run by OICC-RVN.

At least monthly Rear Admiral Bartlett would make a trip from

Chapter XXXIV

DaNang to Saigon to meet personally with the OICC bosses as well as MACV, the Army command and COMNAVFORV, the top Navy command in-country. In spite of his flight schedule with all the "heavy hitters" he always managed to set aside one day for a visit to the Seabee teams in the field. We always looked forward to Admiral Bartlett's visits since it provided us with an opportunity to show off some of our team's accomplishments. These Seabee teams comprised of one officer and 12 enlisted men often accomplished some amazing construction projects. They included a suspension bridge, a two story 12 room school house, sawmill, complete village water system (well, water tank and distribution system) and numerous roads, schools, clinics, orphanages and bridges. In addition Jim Bartlett was a very personable individual and one who could put anyone at ease. He was an avid gardener and had his own vegetable plot outside his "hooch" at China Beach where he grew all sorts of vegetables. When he visited a Seabee team site he frequently found a similar vegetable garden near the camp. At that point everything stopped while the Admiral and the Seabee who took care of the garden discussed "farming."

Another real plus for us at the Seabee Team headquarters was the elevated priority we commanded when we requested air transportation for an Admiral. As Officer-In-Charge of the detachment I could request air support from the Army aviation unit at Tan Son Nhut but a Lieutenant Commander really did not draw much water with anyone over there. Usually the best we could do for our troops was to get a slot on a Caribou log flight or maybe an Air Force C-123. We rarely got our own chopper. As a matter of fact most all of our air support came from Air America, the State Dept/CIA sponsored "civilian" air line that operated throughout Southeast Asia. But when we requested air support for Admiral Bartlett we not only got our own chopper but also a gun ship to provide security. And the helicopters flew at our direction. We did not have to bother with trying to fit into the Army's logistic flight schedule. It really proved to be beneficial to know people in high places.

While he was eager to visit the teams, Admiral Bartlett made it clear that he only wanted to see two teams during his time with us. This was actually a very practical constraint. Even with dedicated air support it ate up most of the day to visit two teams. Since they were scattered throughout the lower three Corps areas the amount of travel time was significant. And Admiral Bartlett always wanted to see their project sites and also visit with the Seabees. Consequently, visits to two team sites pretty much filled the day.

One such visit in August of '68 involved a team site north of Saigon followed by a second team southwest of Saigon on the Cambodian border. I decided we should return to Tan Son Nhut at midday and have lunch at the Seabee House before making the flight to the second team. Everything seemed to go smoothly in the morning and we returned to Tan Son Nhut about noon. The Seabee house was an old Vietnamese three story villa just a few blocks from one of the airfield gates, which we rented for billeting all of the headquarters personnel. It had high masonry walls all around and a large open area where we could park our vehicles as well as a convenient place for our own generator which was used for house power. In addition, we had a roof top bar and a good sized dining area and galley. At this particular time we had just employed a new cook and our corpsman, "Doc" King was in charge of the galley. The female Chinese cook and Doc were both still in the "shakedown cruise" portion of their working relationship, as Doc had not been on board but a few weeks at that time. But as our senior detachment "medical officer" his first collateral duty was to look after the galley and be sure the new cook maintained some acceptable level of sanitation. Doc was also the titular "mess caterer" and he developed the menus together with the cook and the resources of our pantry. This was sometimes touch and go as commissary resupply through NavForV was now and then a little sporadic. Orders on their standard commissary listing frequently were only partially filled with the other items marked NIS (not in stock) or NC (not carried) which meant that it wouldn't do any good to order it next time either as it was no longer in their inventory. But our cook did quite a bit of food shopping, mainly fruits and vegetables, on the local Vietnamese market. This had a double benefit, the produce was fresher and the cost savings were significant. Our cook probably saved us many times the cost of her employment with her local market shopping.

Even so, there were some coordination and communication actions that still needed to be ironed out between Doc and the cook.

In this particular instance the cook apparently was never informed of our plan to have lunch with the Admiral at the Seabee House. Although the Admiral's party only consisted of six of us — and admittedly we were a bit late getting to the Seabee House, arriving about 1230 — the cook was essentially washed up when we arrived. Doc made it clear that she would have to get lunch on the table right away but her first reaction was a big Chinese hissy-fit. After a couple of minutes of high pitched hollers and shouts things settled down and pots and pans began to rattle. Doc got our table set and we had iced tea and a horse cock sandwich on wonder bread

Chapter XXXIV

(which we never ate at the Seabee House as locally baked French bread was available everywhere in Viet Nam. That the commissary even provided a doughy white wonder bread was a surprise to me.) But about the time we finished our sandwich the cook come out of the kitchen with steaming hot bowls of soup for each of us. It was a sort of vegetable beef soup and pretty tasty.

After our lunch we headed back to the chopper pad at Tan Son Nhut and I made apologies to Admiral Bartlett for our sorry luncheon. He graciously said not to worry about it, as it was a good bit better than the alternative which usually was C-Rations. But he did make the comment that the hot soup the cook came up with was pretty tasty.

We toured the second Seabee Team site and returned to Tan Son Nhut late that afternoon where Admiral Bartlett boarded his executive jet for the flight back to I Corps. When I returned to the Seabee House Doc was waiting for me. I assumed to try to explain the dick-up about lunch. Instead he asked how the admiral liked the soup. I related the admiral's comments and Doc asked if I thought it was o.k. I admitted that it was, but also qualified my comments with the fact that I pretty much liked anything when anybody else did the cooking. I also asked why he was so concerned about the soup. After a bit of hemming and hawing Doc said the cook had been pretty flustered with the noontime flap and she was also still learning her way around the kitchen, so to speak. In her haste to make a soup she grabbed a couple of cans of dog food and used that for the meat portion of the soup. So instead of vegetable beef we probably ate vegetable horse meat soup!

Over the next several years I corresponded with Admiral Bartlett a few times but I wanted to wait until we met before I made a confession about the "good soup." Unfortunately, we never did cross paths again. On the other hand the cans of dog food have printed on the label, "fit for human consumption." I guess we can attest to that.

Chapter XXXV

Sleeping On Watch

EVERYONE WHO HAS BEEN part of the military has probably spent time, maybe a lot of time, on watch. It begins in boot camp and in one form or another it never ends. From seaman recruit to CNO, one element of every billet is to spend time "on watch." Admittedly, it is usually the non-rates or lower rated petty officers who actually wear the guard belt, carry a weapon and walk a post. And that is the group I single out for this discussion.

As a white hat I stood my share of fire, ramp and security watches during the Korean War. None of it actually in Korea but in the U.S. and Atlantic areas. In boot camp everyone is indoctrinated in the eleven general orders of a sentry. Some of us actually made an attempt to memorize them but the principal guide line was to walk your post and not to go to sleep! In all honesty that not going to sleep part was sometimes the biggest challenge. Standing the mid-watch on the seaplane ramp at Quonset Point, R.I. in December, with the wind coming in across Narragansett Bay was about as cold as I have ever been in my life. I quickly developed a routine to deal with it. I would make one round of the aircraft parking area and then pick a strategically located P-2V patrol plane and crawl up in the observer's seat in the nose of the aircraft. From that vantage point I could watch any vehicle traffic that might come onto the ramp as well as any surface traffic on the bay. I also had a view of the doorway from the hangar in case the JOOD might want to make an unannounced check of the post watches. But best of all it was out of the wind and provided a somewhat comfortable seat. Of course there was no heat in the aircraft but compared to the temperature outside it was right near comfortable. In fact it was so nice the biggest challenge was to keep from nodding off. Men could be shot for sleeping on watch, according to Navy scuttlebutt. And even though there was no shooting going on in Rhode Island, other than the mafia, we were essentially at war in Korea. We all took that no sleeping on watch requirement quite seriously. Between my hourly walks around the ramp and the intervening warm up time in the aircraft I managed to both keep an eye on the government property and to keep from freezing.

Years later, as a commissioned officer in a Seabee battalion my duty requirements as OOD involved checking the watches to insure they were alert. This was in the early 60's in Okinawa. Even though there was little threat of hostile action the ongoing incursions onto the base by the Okinawa "stealie-boys" made our security watches a real necessity. Not only would they break into warehouses and shops they even removed parts from vehicles in our parking area if we did not maintain a roving security guard. Even though the troops were aware of the incursions by the "stealie-boys" it was still a constant battle to keep some of the watches alert. It was not unusual to quietly walk up to a man on watch and find him with his chin resting on his chest. On one such incident I have to admit I admired the young Seabees inventiveness. When I spoke to him, and I'm sure interrupted his dozing, he quickly said: "amen" and then raised his head. After all who can chastise a trooper for praying on watch?

In one of General Patton's more memorable speeches he emphasized the need for constantly remaining alert. In his words he said: "(For) a man, to continue breathing, (he) must be alert at all times. If not, sometime a German son-of-a-bitch will sneak up behind him and beat him to death with a sock full of shit." He went on to say: "There are four hundred neatly marked graves somewhere in Sicily, all because one man went to sleep on his job. But they are German graves, for we caught the bastards asleep before they did us."

Obviously the need to remain alert is a paramount element of military security and it begins at the guard post. During Viet Nam there was obviously a heightened level of security as one never really knew who was friendly and who was enemy. In fact, the same individual could sometimes be both depending on the time of day. During the early 60's, 1964 to be precise, the U.S. military involvement in Viet Nam consisted mainly of province advisory teams and U.S. Army Special Forces units who were actively involved in the training of the VNSF (Viet Namese Special

Forces). We also had a few Seabee Technical Assistance Teams (STATs) in country which were assigned to the Special Forces, primarily to assist them in developing their "A" team camp sites. The Special Forces "A" teams were comprised of two officers, normally a Capt. and a 1st Lieutenant, together with a team first sergeant, medic, radio operator, and seven other experienced NCO's, mostly weapons specialists. All team members were jump qualified and rangers. Basically they were a dozen trained killers. But in Viet Nam their principal task was training. However this was quite literally "on-the-job" training. All of the "A" teams were located right in the middle of bandit country or on a main supply route of the VC (Viet Cong) and NVA (North Vietnamese Army). That is why the Seabee teams were brought into the picture. Our job was to build a landing strip near the camp so they could be resupplied by fixed wing cargo aircraft as opposed to the Marine helicopters. Early on, the resupply for the team at Nam Dong was entirely by helicopter. There was a vehicular trail from Route 1 (the main coastal roadway through the country) and it was passable with our military vehicles but only part time. In two places just north of the camp it was necessary to ford the rivers. During periods of high water it was impassable. And that could be for two to three months at a time depending on the season. That was our secondary tasking, build two bridges at those locations.

In addition to being located in hostile country the "A" team camps were all alike with respect to their configuration. In the center was the U.S. only zone where all the U.S. personnel, Army and Seabees, were located as well as the comm center. Outside of that was the inner perimeter which contained the sick bay, armory, chow hall, galley, etc. and the inner perimeter defense fighting holes and mortar pits. In addition to all the U.S. personnel the inner perimeter included the Nung Chinese guard contingent. These were in effect the bodyguards for the Special Forces. As I understood it the Nungs were a clan of Chinese who had been mercenaries for centuries. At one time they had been the protectors of the mandarins. Later they did the same for high ranking Nationalist Chinese. Following the communist takeover China they immigrated to French Indo China and worked for the French Foreign Legion. After Dien Bien Phu they moved south again and eventually became a security force for the Special Forces. The main element of the Nungs services was the fact that they were exceedingly loyal and could be trusted. This was in addition to being a quality fighting force. As mentioned earlier this loyalty element was pretty much hit or miss with the Vietnamese troops, even though they were part of the VNSF. At any rate the Nungs were part of the inner perimeter and they provided the 24 hour security for this area. They also went on patrols and search and destroy missions with the Special Forces. Outside the inner perimeters was a much larger area called the outer perimeter. This defined the camp limits and housed the VNSF. Their fighting positions were just inside the wire. The "Nung Platoon" probably numbered about 30 individuals. The leader of the Nung contingent was a fellow named Le Sa Tung. In practically all aspects he resembled the more well known Chinaman Mao Sa Tung. Both were fairly short and stout, both had receding hair lines and neither of them smiled very much. In the case of Le, he was a superb troop leader. His fighters were responsible for the inner perimeter security on a 24/7 basis and they carried out that task flawlessly. Their fighting holes were located around the inner perimeter and placed so that there was enfilading fire from at least two positions all the way around the compound. Le frequently held impromptu weapons inspections on his troops as well as doing his own guard post surprise inspections. The Nung organization included several men who were designated sergeant and they were responsible for posting the guards and overseeing their performance, but everyone knew the "Chief Nung", Le, could also show up at any time. This made for a particularly alert guard force and was very reassuring to all of us Uniform-Sierra (U.S.) troops. Both Special Forces and Seabees.

Even in spite of their intense training and close supervision there were once in a great while some slip-ups. In one particular case one of the Nung guards on the inner perimeter was found to be asleep on watch. I'm not sure who discovered the miscreant, Le or one of the sergeants, but that made little difference as Le was the one who dealt with the problem. And he did so immediately and quite severely.

Within the inner perimeter there was a "facility" I had never encountered before. It was a hole in the ground that was about 15 feet deep and lined with a series of five oil drums with the tops and bottoms cut out. Stacked on top of each other they made a reinforced tube that terminated at ground level and rested on a gravel base at the bottom so as to facilitate drainage. The Special Forces X.O. told me this was sometimes used in the interrogation of VC prisoners. I never asked for an explanation as to just how it was used, but I soon learned of at least one method.

The Nung who was found asleep on watch was a young man somewhere between 15 and 25 years of age and like most of the Nungs rather short and slender. After a heated one way conversation in Chinese where Le did practically all of the talking and the guard kept looking at his boots and shaking his head, Le had someone bring him a rope. He tied one end around the guard's chest and then walked him to the pit. Two or three Nungs held the bitter end of the line and the guard was lowered into the pit with only his head and shoulders above ground. Le then put a hand grenade in each of the guard's fists and pulled the pins. Then the guard was lowered to the bottom.

At this point the guard had two options. Theoretically he could toss the grenades out of the pit with just enough arc that they would come to rest on the surface adjacent to the pit and explode there or he could hold the spoons in place until he was pulled from the pit.
Neither option was attractive.

If he tried to toss the grenades out he was first impeded by a lack of movement. The diameter of a drum is only about 24 inches so the toss would have to be using the forearm only. Plus the trajectory would have to be perfect, only a few degrees off of vertical. To get the grenade to fall outside the pit opening the toss would have to start from one side of the pit and just clear the opposite side at the top. The odds of making such a perfect toss — and doing it twice — probably range from zero to negative infinity. Any number of factors could result in the armed grenade falling back into the pit and exploding there. All things considered just holding the spoons in place quickly became the better course of action.

But that was not an easy option. To begin with the guard had been awake for some time and now he was going to have to remain awake and alert for another extended period. It is not known if Le told him how long his time in the pit would be but as it turned out it was 24 hours. The guard had to hold both grenades quite firmly to keep the spoons in place. There would not be any dozing on this watch. During this time in the pit the guard was not given any food or water. Actually a moot point as he was unable to grasp anything else anyhow. Bodily functions were controlled by mother nature and probably came into play rather quickly, given the circumstances. The metal cylinder formed by the oil drums provided no features where the guard could place the grenade and spoon into a nook or cranny that would hold the spoon in place. In short the only option was to stay awake and keep a good grip on the grenade and the spoon.

The day passed quickly for the Seabees as we were out of the camp working on projects during the day. When we returned in the late afternoon we got a quick sitrep (situation report) on the guard; i.e. no explosions, yet. During the evening hours everyone seemed to be preoccupied one way or another but we were all waiting for an explosion. The subject of how long he was going to keep him in the pit was brought up but the

Chapter XXXV

C.O. of the Special Forces team said the Nung method of operation was theirs alone and no one should even raise the question.

The night passed uneventfully and we all rolled out at 0500, had breakfast and went to our job sites. Later that morning Le went to the pit and had some of his troops haul the guard to the surface. He took the grenades from the guard and dropped them in the pit where they exploded. Actually the explosion was quite muffled by the pit characteristics. After another brief lecture by Le the guard was allowed to go to his hootch and get some sleep.

This episode certainly impressed the young Nung guard but it also made a big impact on the Seabees and the Special Forces troops, as well.

Chapter XXXVI

A Letter From Momma

BACK IN THE DARK AGES, the 1960's to be precise, letters were the principal means of communication for deployed military troops. A few locations had access to MARS (Military Amateur Radio Station) radio facilities but those were not as effective as advertised. To begin with both parties usually had to go to the local area MARS station and remember to say "over" at the end of each transmission. Pre-arranging a radio time was also more of a hassle than anticipated. Some military families would record messages on tape cassettes and mail those back and forth but still the old time honored letter seemed to be the most reliable. Computer e-mail and cell phones have pretty much taken over these days but letters from home were a highlight years ago.

They certainly were for CS2 Gnader who was one of MCB-NINE'S commissarymen (cooks & bakers) during our Okinawa deployment in '63. Gnader was something of a character. His home town was a small place in Tennessee. He was what was described as a "career second class", but in his case that was due to his own preference as opposed to not being able to pass the first class test. He wore four hash marks on his jumper signifying 16 years of service plus, and according to him he had no intention of making first class let alone chief petty officer. Consequently he made it a point never to take the first class test. If he were to do that and get promoted he would automatically end up as a watch captain and have to give up his night baker position. From his standpoint being the night baker was a perfect assignment. He had

Chapter XXXVI

a helper but he was not in charge of a number of people. He reported to the galley late in the evening and did all his baking overnight. He usually secured about 0600 in the morning. With this schedule he avoided most all of the military requirements: musters, duty sections, daily quarters, etc. and was able to concentrate on his first love — baking. And he was a great baker. He kept the battalion well supplied with bread, rolls, pastries and some really delicious cakes. He was also quite good at decorating the cakes.

He was probably in his late 30's, never married, always smiling which exposed his missing teeth. Naturally the Navy had provided him with bridges for his missing teeth but he chose not to use them. Gnader probably was ahead of most of us in that he was apparently fully satisfied with his lot in life. He liked being in the Navy, he liked his duty with the Seabees, and he really liked his job of night baker. Consequently, from his viewpoint, life was good. He was friends with everybody but I don't think he palled around with anyone. In fact I doubt that he went on liberty very often even though he had watch standers liberty by virtue of being a cook. Once you got to know him it became clear early on that the most important person in his life was his mother back in Tennessee. And the highlight of his week was when he would get "a letter from momma." He liked to share the news from home with others and that is how Gnader and I became friends.

Being the equipment company (A Company) commander for the battalion, the only time I came in contact with him was during my galley visits while standing OOD watch. As the duty officer it was essential to sample at least one meal in the crews mess during the watch and report on quality, quantity and "in accordance with the menu" categories. These were more or less perfunctory exercises as our Seabee galleys normally have a long standing reputation of being "good feeders." But I usually made it a point of sampling the breakfast meal. To be honest I always hoped they would be serving S.O.S for breakfast. A tray full of S.O.S and a big mug of Navy coffee would keep you going all day long.

But at the breakfast hour Gnader was just about to come off watch. He was done baking and generally stood around behind the serving line with a mug of coffee saying hello to everybody. Including the duty officers. The galley had a small table and two chairs set aside for the duty officer (I suspect we may have ruined some of the troop's appetite if we had barged in on them during a meal) and I invited Gnader to join me and finish his coffee, which he was pleased to do. After all, a 16 year second class was not about to be intimidated by a "jaygee." I was about to ask him how things were going in the galley but I never got the chance. He let me know right away that he had recently received a "letter from momma" and asked if I would like to hear it. Being from a small town myself and having experienced many such letters from my home I didn't think there was much chance of getting too personal. Besides, he obviously wanted to pass the good news on to someone. Even if it was an officer.

Between gulps of strong "mid-watch" coffee Gnader proceeded to read me the news from his part of Tennessee, as seen by his mother. As expected there were several items concerning home folks, each of whom he clarified with a relationship explanation. The girl who was expecting a baby was a cousin, the fellow who had the tractor accident was a neighbor, the fellows who were arrested by the sheriff last Saturday were all guys he had gone to school with, and so on. But the one item I remember specifically from our first meeting was the news that the kitchen sink had become discolored and a little rusty and his mother indicated she was going to have to save up some money and buy a new sink "directly". Gnader informed me that as soon as he got off watch he was going over to our battalion post office and was going to send his mother a money order so she could buy a new sink right away. I'm sure he did. But that was generally the tenor of the news from "momma". Once in a while there would be word of somebody getting shot — not accidentally — and there were a few instances of people being shot and killed. Apparently Gnader was from a town that was not unlike the Hatfield and McCoy area.

As the deployment proceeded I think both Gnader and I looked forward to our breakfast coffee and news break once or twice each month. Later on, when I had to be up late at night for equipment mount out via air lifts from Kadena Air Force Base or some such activity, I would drop by the galley in the middle of the night for coffee and a doughnut or pastry (whatever was just out of the oven) and a visit with Gnader. Naturally the latest news from momma was also provided.

I suspect I may have been the only person in the battalion who listened to his newsy letters more than once. But that was just fine. As I said earlier I was pretty much accustomed to that sort of news from home myself so it was somewhat like home town visit for me.

Our Okinawa deployment was completed in Dec. '63 and the battalion returned to Port Hueneme, Calif. Our next deployment began about April '64. Even though the battalion again deployed to Okinawa as the back-up battalion, I took my Seabee Team, STAT-0904, to Viet-Nam to work for Army Special Forces units and later for the State Department doing civic action construction. In November '64 we were relieved in Quang-Tri province and the CBPAC detachment in Saigon arranged for us to return to Okinawa to rejoin the battalion before returning to Port Hueneme. In a way just getting back to the battalion was almost like being home again. We flew into Kadena from Tan Son Nhut on a C-130, arriving about 2200. I was surprised to see a small crowd from the battalion there at Kadena to meet us. Officers, Chiefs, friends of team members and even our new battalion C.O., Cdr. Dick Anderson showed up.

Other than personal gear, which wasn't much for each man, we quickly offloaded the team gear and made the short ride over to Camp Kinser. The galley had set up a "nite rats" line for our team and we were quite pleased over that. There were a good many food items we had not seen for the past seven months. As I recall one of my mechanics, "Tommy" Thompson made a head of lettuce and a quart of milk his first meal.

Of course Gnader knew of our scheduled return and he baked us a special welcome home cake. The icing held the words "WELCOME HOME STAT 0904 AND MR. OLSEN." As usual the cake was delicious.

And oh yes, I got to hear the latest news from Tennessee via Gnaders most recent letter from momma.

It really was great to be "home".

Chapter XXXVII

Kami Kaze

*K*EN MAXWELL WAS NOT very tall, only about 5'-2" and was described by some southerners as "no bigger than a bar of soap after a hard days washing." But in all respects he was an outstanding officer.

I met him in Oct. '62 when I reported aboard my first battalion MCB-NINE. He was the battalion supply officer, a LCdr. and older than most officers in his grade. That was understandable since he had served as an enlisted man, actually a boiler tender, aboard a destroyer in the Pacific during WWII. After the war he took advantage of the G.I. Bill and enrolled at Ole Miss where he earned a business degree. Sometime later he again joined the Navy with a commission in the Supply Corps. Along the way he married his long time sweetheart and they had several children.

In the battalion Ken was respected and admired by officers and enlisted alike. He became the "father confessor" to many Seabees. This was not only due to the fact that our battalion chaplain at the time was pretty sorry but most likely due to the fact that Ken was understanding, knowledgeable and had a practical background of the Navy, both officer and enlisted. As such he knew firsthand the trials and tribulations as well as the concerns of both communities. In addition he recognized the limitations or boundaries of what was possible in the Navy system. He also had another positive attribute, he had a wry sense of humor and was always good for a laugh.

As has been mentioned Okinawa was a great liberty port. It seemed

Chapter XXXVII

as if everybody in the battalion made the best of it. Ken Maxwell was no exception. But he was one of the group known as "straight arrows." They might go into town and have a few beers with the bar girls but it stopped there. They did not patronize the cat houses.

But LCdr Maxwell did have one weakness. He likes the hotsi baths. His night on the town usually consisted of a haircut at the Paris barbershop, one or two beers, a hotsi bath and a taxi back to the camp. You could almost guarantee he would be back from town by 2200 (10:00 p.m.) During our time on Okinawa he probably hit every hotsi bath house in Koza and most all of them in the center of the island. But one particular bath house in Koza was very memorable for Ken and hilarious to the rest of us in the wardroom. Following one of his weekly "nights on the town" — usually a Friday — most all of the battalion officers were already in the wardroom Saturday morning when LCdr Maxwell came in for his breakfast. I don't recall how it began but someone got him talking about his latest hotsi bath. At this point he surprised us all by declaring "I ain't ever going back there again." This was quite a departure from his normal "after action report." Usually he would brag about each and every bath house and highly recommend it to the rest of the wardroom.

Of course we were all intrigued by this unanticipated announcement so we began by peppering him with questions.

Were you overcharged?
No.
Wasn't it clean? (This would be a real rarity in Japan)
No.
Did you get propositioned? (It never did happen in the legitimate bath houses.)
No
Were the girls ugly?
No
Well what was the problem?

Ken began by telling us precisely which bath house he patronized and went on to say that his nasan (bath house girl) was older than most and rather short and had a stocky build. This was not all that unusual even though the majority of the bath house girls were young attractive Japanese girls. Ken was a friendly sort and when the massage session began he tried to engage the nasan in conversation. But her command of English was somewhat limited and Ken's Japanese, like most all of us, was practically nil. But he did not stop trying to have at least some dialog with her. Finally he asked if she was married.

She answered, "No, husband dead."

He was about to say he was sorry to hear that when she went on to proudly announce: "Husband kami-kaze." It's a bit difficult for Americans to understand how a suicide pilot can be held in such high regard in Japan but there is no doubt that it still is an important part of family pride in that country.

(Personally I subscribe to Gen. Patton's philosophy: "Make that other poor dumb bastard give his life for his country.") But I digress. Remember now that Ken had been a white hat on a destroyer throughout the battle for Okinawa, and his battle station was as a gunner on a twin 30 caliber gun mount. As such, he had experienced a number of kami-kaze attacks during the Okinawa campaign and probably had sent thousands of rounds in their direction.

In any case he rolled to one side, pointed both his forefingers outward as if they were gun barrels and said: "Me — sailor boy, ACK ACK ACK ACK ACK!"

The nasan did not say a word but she rolled Ken back on his stomach and according to him she proceeded to pound the hell out of him.

Like Ken said later: "I ain't ever going back their again!"

Chapter XXXVIII

This Island Sucks

THE ARCHIPELAGO OF DIEGO GARCIA is located about seven degrees south of the equator and 100 miles south southwest of the southern tip of India. Practically every Seabee who served on active duty sometime during the period 1970 through 1983 knows of the island first hand as it was the principal deployment site for battalions for many of these years.

Officially titled the British Indian Ocean Territory, or BIOT, the island commander is a Brit and they still are the legal "landlords." But in the early 70's an agreement was reached between governments which allowed the U.S. to construct a communications station on the island in order to improve radio contact with fleet units operating in the Indian Ocean area. Immediately after the signing of the agreement the Seabees dispatched a recon party from Davisville, R.I. to survey the site in order to plan the deployment of the construction forces as well as to locate sites for the communication facilities, the Seabee camp, favorable beach landing areas, etc. Shortly after the team's return to Davisville an advanced party was deployed to Diego with the task of establishing a Seabee camp site for the battalion. All of the early deployments were by surface ship, LST's and mike boats, as there were no facilities for supporting aircraft. The "over the beach" landing with construction equipment and building supplies was essentially the same as Seabees had been doing since 1942. But the big difference between WWII, Korea and Viet Nam, as compared with

Diego Garcia, was that no one was firing at the Seabees who came ashore on Diego.

There were some island inhabitants, local islanders who operated a copra plantation on the island for many years. Their facilities and crop areas were mainly on the eastern side of the atoll while the planned Seabee construction site was on the western leg of the U shaped atoll. A few years later the British government relocated these islanders to another island in the Seychelles.

At any rate the landing of supplies and equipment came off without any major "hiccups." The campsite was quickly developed and work on the comm. station facilities was soon underway. Work on the Seabee camp was pretty straight forward and simple; strong back huts with corrugated metal roofs, frame construction for offices, shop and storage as well as the EM club and a couple PEB (pre-engineering bldgs) structures for warehouses, etc. But the communications facilities were considerably more sophisticated. Dousing some of their materials in salt water could prove to be embarrassing, expensive and time consuming as practically all replacement items were months away. To eliminate this possibility a deep water pier was requested. This would allow commercial and Navy freighters to tie up and offload in the usual manner as opposed to lightering everything from ship-to-shore. In short order a pier was authorized and built but the need for emergency resupply also became evident. The ability to fly military cargo aircraft to the island to deliver critical items and keep the work on schedule was part of the proposal for a short expeditionary runway but the capability to medevac injured or ill personnel right away made the argument even more convincing.

In no time a C-130 capable runway was completed.

About the same time the element of "mission creep" began to develop. The original communication station was expanded to provide some "limited" support facilities that would allow the island to be a divert field for Navy and Marine Corps aircraft operating in that part of the Indian Ocean. That meant that there would be a need for a longer and heavier runway to support the jet aircraft, additional parking aprons, taxiways, cross-taxiways, jet fuel storage, hangars, maintenance shops, a POL buoy in the lagoon with fuel transfer pipelines to the beach area and fuel storage tanks. Actually an entire tank farm would be required to store all the various types of fuel products and of course the pier would have to be made longer, wider and stronger.

In no time it became apparent that the need to expand the aerial

Chapter XXXVIII 139

resupply capability so a C-5 capable runway, taxiways and aprons was soon in the works.

You see where this is going, don't you?

Seemingly before you know it the Air Force is flying B-52 missions off the island and the Navy and Marine Corps are anchoring pre-positioned supply ships in the lagoon.

By 1983 the construction requirements on Diego were expanding beyond what Seabee battalions could provide, given their deployment schedules and other Navy related construction requirements. As a result the work began to be transferred to the OICC (Officer in Charge of Construction) and construction contracts were awarded to civilian contractors. At the same time the Seabee effort on the island began to draw down.

In any case things were getting entirely too civilized for a deployment site for Seabees. We had long ago passed the exciting part of the work; deploy to an island site, set up a camp, construct facilities with minimal outside support, innovate every day — both on the job and off, etc. In other words do all the fun things. Now there was an active public works activity on the island to take care of maintenance and operations plus an OICC to administer construction contracts using civilian firms. Things were so tame even the Air Force was on site. That's for sure time for the Seabees to "Get outa Dodge."

One of the last full battalion deployments to Diego Garcia was made by MCB-ONE from Gulfport, Miss. They had the usual heavy work load to be completed during their tour on the island but the battalion had been given stepped up manning and as usual they were augmented by detachments from every other deployed battalion, both Atlantic and Pacific. Most of their jobs were sizable projects but they also had a number of small "pot boiler" taskings.

One instance of work on a small project involved a Seabee utilitiesman (UT) working on a pump on a pipeline in an out- lying area. As usual it was quite hot and humid and the situation down in the pump pit was even more miserable as there was not a breath of fresh air in the pit, much less any breeze. The UT was wringing wet with sweat, somewhat aggravated because the work was not going well, thirsty and getting tired of wiping the sweat out of his eyes so he could see what he was doing. About this time someone stuck his head over the edge of the pit and asked, "How's it going?"

For years Diego Garcia had been an attractive trip for everyone in the Navy-providing they had never visited there before. In this case the visitor was a line Rear Admiral who had apparently completed whatever official duties he had on the island and was spending the rest of his day walking around the island sightseeing. His amiable tour around the area was ended abruptly when the Seabee answered, without looking up, "Not worth a shit."

"What seems to be the problem?" Asked the Admiral.

"Can't get this damn pump to work." Replied the Seabee.

At this point the Admiral apparently thought it would be better to change the subject if he was going to engage the Seabee in conversation, so he asked, "How long have you been on Diego Garcia?"

"Five and a half months" was the immediate reply.

"How do you like out here?"

Even quicker the Seabee replied, "This island sucks."

Although Admirals are familiar with the plain spoken assessments of the troops, he was slightly taken aback by the blunt and uncomplimentary evaluation by the Seabee. Even so, he attempted to find a positive element so he said, "Really, but it can't be all bad. How's the chow?"

Seabee galleys have been noted for good food and ample quantities ever since WWII and the meals at Diego Garcia were generally rated quite high. The Admiral had eaten several meals on the island and was impressed with the food service so he figured he would be on safe ground with this question.

Not so. The Seabee quickly answered "Chow sucks."

"That's too bad," replied the Admiral. "It seemed pretty good to me yesterday. How's the fishing?"

"Fishing sucks."

"Is that a fact? Is there any other recreation here on the island?"

"All of it sucks."

The Admiral then figured he had at least one positive element he could count on when he said, "I suppose you must spend most of your spare time at the EM club. They keep the beer pretty cold there I'm told."

"The beer is British and it sucks."

At this point the Admiral had pretty much decided there was little chance he could find anything the Seabee would look at favorably. So he said "You don't seem to care too much for this place, do you?"

The Seabee shot back, "Sure don't. Everything on this damn island sucks. — Except this friggin pump — but it's going to be sucking too when I get done with it."

Thanks to Cdr. Burns Whittaker for the initial input on this story.

Chapter XXXIX

Hello Seabee

"P-FLY" OR "FLY" was the way team members normally addressed him but his proper name was John I. Peffley, the I stood for Ivan. At the time he was a second class utilities man, UT2, but in addition to being an outstanding plumber he had a wealth of other talents. He was a great cook, a super salesman; he had a special affinity for animals and was the unofficial public relations man for our Seabee Team. His salesman and PR talents may have been an outgrowth of some early training at the Peffley Ford dealership near Dayton, Ohio. Although he was not exceptionally tall he was physically quite impressive. Built like a refrigerator, he already had a receding blond hairline and a continual smile.

Even though he was in his late twenties he was still unmarried. He liked to say he was married to the Navy. But he managed to find time for the ladies every now and then. At the time our Seabee Team had been sent to an Army Special Forces "A" team camp in the mountains south of Hue, Viet Nam. We had a team house in Hue and a considerable amount of our gear and supplies were still there. Since our projects for the Special Forces didn't involve any plumbing I assigned Fly to be our team house watchman in Hue until we returned. For some reason I had to return briefly to Hue to take care of some matter with the Military Assistance Command in Vietnam (MACV) headquarters for I Corps. Before I could do any business with the U.S. Army I found it necessary to run a few co's (Vietnames for girls) out of the team house. Fly had only been there a couple of weeks but he already had acquired a harem. My guess is that they were probably back in the house before I had returned to the Special Forces camp at Nam Dong.

But in spite of a few minor defects in his standards of conduct, Fly was a great team member and a continual morale booster. More than anything he always seemed to come up with something that would keep us laughing.

Our tasking at the Special Forces camp at Nam Dong was pretty straight forward. We were to build two bridges over some small rivers which would allow all weather traffic from the camp site out to Route 1 on the coast. Route 1 was the main line of communication from Saigon to Hanoi even though it stopped at the DMZ, (De-militarized zone) between North and South Viet Nam. Shortly after we arrived the Special Forces C.O., Capt. John Eddy, asked if we could carve out an area adjacent to the camp that would allow a Caribou, a small twin engine Army cargo plane, to land and take off. Without a reliable road system or landing field their only resupply was by the Marine choppers. But the Marines had other priority missions so the Special Forces log flights were more or less opportune lifts, whenever the chopper flight schedule would permit. There was plenty of sand and aggregate around and an old French steam roller was also on site. My mechanic, CM3 "Johnny" Johnson, fell in love with the steam roller, soon had it running and would not allow anyone else to operate it. So we added the expeditionary landing field to our project list.

One other major element of our tasking was the MedCAP operations in the nearby villages. MedCAP is Medical Civic Action Program. My team corpsman, HM2 "Doc" Necas was provided with an allowance of medications to be dispensed to the locals when he would hold a clinic in their village. Doc always drew a crowd and the locals were very appreciative of his efforts — even if they failed to follow the directions he gave them through our interpreter. The MedCAP program was a big part of our "hearts and minds" effort to enhance our relationship with the locals, and probably the most effective element of the entire program.

The "hearts and minds" effort was an important part of the Special Forces program as well. Shortly before we arrived they had collected all the brass from their firing range and taken it to Da Nang where it was melted down and recast as a large bell. The team then presented it to the local Buddhist congregation for use in their temple. According to Capt. Eddy that made them many many "brownie points." Even so, we still had to come up with other efforts to endear ourselves with the neighbors. Capt Eddy and 1st Lt. Hugh Sproul, the C.O. & X.O. of the Special Forces team, and I developed a plan to provide water wells and hand pumps for several villages along the roadway to the coast. As is frequently the case with civic action projects others come up with the idea but it falls back on the Seabees to do the work. But that's all right. We're not only good at it we are faster and better than other outfits at this sort of thing.

A total of six villages were identified as locations for the water wells. Most of the villages were inhabited by native Vietnamese but we also had two of the nearby hamlets that were comprised of Montegnards, or mountain tribesmen.

Previously the villagers would obtain their water from the nearby river or streams or from a very basic type of catchment facility. So the well and pump would be quite an improvement for them. In addition to providing a measure of filtration the well would also be much more convenient and a boon to all villagers. Since we were located in a river basin it was a pretty straight forward operation to install a well. Drilling to reach water was not a factor. After selecting a well site we would hand dig a hole to below the summer water table elevation, case the well with one meter diameter reinforced concrete pipe which we made in camp, provide a gravel filter base at the bottom of the well and finally install a reinforced concrete cap and an old style hand pump as used to be seen on farms and country schools everywhere. The hand pumps were provided from a USAID program administered by a civilian in Hue.

Since we now had a plumbing project, more or less, I brought P-Fly out from Hue and put him in charge of the project. The first order of business was to get agreement from the village chiefs as well as to solicit some free labor from each of them in the form of manpower to do the actual digging. Fly and Ding-Dong, our Vietnamese interpreter, made the initial contacts. After some extended negotiations with the village chiefs and elders, and numerous glasses of tea, they eventually reached agreements on all of the wells. Actually the offer of a well was accepted right away once they understood what it was that was being proposed. But the translation of the conversations both ways sometimes got a little far afield. Another factor that had to be considered was the amount of time dedicated to the negotiation. In the oriental mind the discussions on a monumental project such as this could not be rushed and all aspects of the work had to be completely thrashed out before making the final decision. And they were — six times over! The next stumbling block was the location of the well. Since all the villages were along the river bottom the well site was not particularly crucial. But without fail, each of the village chiefs wanted it to be near his house, at least initially. Usually that was not a preferred well site so it took some time to get agreement on a more advantageous (from a well drilling viewpoint) location. On these occasions P-Fly was quick to point out to the village chiefs that they probably would not like to have all these people around their houses at all hours of day and night. The chiefs all saw the wisdom of that and P-Fly eventually managed to site the wells as he saw fit.

The construction effort was pretty straight forward. P-Fly, Ding-Dong and a few shovels all loaded into a weapons carrier (3/4 ton truck) and drove to the site. The chiefs provided men to do the digging and they dug a one meter diameter hole about three to five meters deep which was below the summer (dry season) water table. The reinforced concrete pipe sections were set to case the well hole and a concrete cap and the farm pump were installed. In all cases the construction itself went rather quickly. When compared with the negotiating phase the construction was a piece of cake.

And the locals were very appreciative. They quickly became accustomed to using the pump. The women of the villages were the main users. Their trip to the water point was now shortened considerably and they no longer had to wade into the river to get their water.

During the construction P-Fly would converse constantly with the village chief or "head-man." He would quickly ingratiate himself to the chief and villagers in spite of his lack of a language ability. After the initial meetings and the start of construction the interpreter, Ding-Dong, did not go to the well sites. Only P-Fly. He seemed to get along with all the village chiefs exceptionally well. But that was not surprising as he got along with everybody. It did not matter if they met in a Vietnamese jungle, a Marine Corps bar, a parking lot, a gas station or anywhere else, he could strike up a conversation and develop a rapport with anybody. He had the innate ability to become an instant friend. This would even transcend the different cultures and languages. As the saying goes, "He never met a stranger." So it was with the village chiefs he met. For some reason P-Fly did not pick up much of the local language or dialects, but he did transfer some English to the locals. As it turned out these words and phrases were not what one would consider dinner table conversation but more accurately some Seabee phrases that probably recurred from time to time during the work day. Anxious to please this big smiley Seabee, the chiefs, locals and children all picked up some of his vocabulary.

The wells were installed in villages that were within three or four "klicks" (kilometers) of the Special Forces camp. And as mentioned two of these villages were Montegnard villages. The Montegnard villages had a very formal, and strict, organization which we never fully understood.

Chapter XXXIX

But one only had to know that the village chief was the first, last and only word on a subject. Whatever he decided was totally supported by all villagers.

As expected the construction phase went quite fast. All the materials were on hand or immediately available and the local labor was likewise plentiful. When the work was completed and the wells checked out, I sent P-Fly back to Hue to be custodian of our team house until the team returned.

A short while later the OIC (Officer in Charge) of all Seabee teams in RVN, LCdr Jack Wright, flew up from Saigon to see how things were going. At the time I had the only Seabee team that was still assigned to a Special Forces "A" team camp. As might be expected the accommodations were pretty Spartan. The army's make shift hootches were definitely of the expeditionary variety half in the ground and half above ground. Wrinkle-iron (corrugated) metal roofing and screens around the above ground portion of the structure provided the protection from the elements. We did have metal frame beds but our bedding consisted of our sleeping bags. As one might expect we were not prepared to host visitors. That was not unusual as no one in their right mind, even the Special Forces "C" team members from Da Nang, on their infrequent visits, would stay overnight.

So it was a bit of a surprise when a Marine chopper showed up early one morning, making one of their resupply flights for the team, and Jack Wright hopped out carrying his AWOL bag and announced he would be with us for a couple of days. After some scurrying around Capt. Eddy decided we could give him a rack in the sick bay — sheets and all.

Even with all these luxurious accommodations Jack Wright was not inclined to spend more time in the camp than necessary to he asked me to show him our projects right away. The airfield and the two bridges were near the camp so that was no problem as we could walk to all three projects. Later I put him in one of our weapons carriers and we headed up the road to look at the well and pump installations. We stopped at the first village and had a good look at the well and watched as the locals pumped their containers full and carried them away. The second well was in a Montegnard village. When we arrived there was no one at the pump other than this short, grizzled old Montegnard who was wearing only shorts, flip-flops and a wide brim bush hat that had once belonged to some G.I. He was in the process of pumping water into a metal five gallon can. As soon as he saw us he stopped pumping, stood at attention, took off his hat, made a sweeping bow and said "Hello Seabee — mean mother fucker!"

To be honest I did not know what to say. But Jack saved the day for me when he said: "This has got to be one of Peffley's jobs isn't it?"

Obviously P-Fly's reputation had gone far beyond I-Corps when the folks in Saigon knew about his exploits. Jack gave the old Montegnard a salute and was repaid with a big smile so things seemed to work out all right.

Fortunately I never did receive a request for any of my Seabees to conduct English language training for the locals, as some teams had done. In any case I don't think P-Fly would have been on the short list of possible instructors.

Later on there was a sequel to this episode. After we had completed our work at the "A" team camp we redeployed to Quang-Tri, the most northern province in South Viet Nam. Like all provinces there was a U.S. Military Assistance Advisory Group assigned there and our allocated building and grounds compound was adjacent to the MAAG area.

The MAAG unit dealt mainly with the Vietnamese military in the province while we were involved in performing a civic action type of construction for the local populace. Consequently we seldom had much interaction.

In a way it was good to be out of the jungle and back in town. The jobs were more varied, we could buy some building supplies fairly readily, good French bread was available daily and there was even a Chinese restaurant that we frequented now and then. The MAAG team had been in place for some time and the locals were accustomed to seeing U.S. military driving around the town. As always the small children would run to the roadside to wave and yell, "Hello — O.K." when a U.S. vehicle passed by. They did the same to all the Seabee equipment.

About a month after arriving in Quang-Tri I was summoned to the province senior advisors office. This was a U.S. Army major. I had made a courtesy call shortly after we moved to the province but we had little interface after that. Consequently I was in the dark as to the reason for the summons. When I walked into his office it became apparent that the major was not all that happy. He lit into me right away and said something like, "It's your damn Seabees that caused all of this. We never had any problems before you came to town. I want it stopped and I want it stopped right now!" I was totally in the dark and it probably showed as he went on to say, "Don't play dumb with me. You caused it and I want you to fix it and I want it fixed today. Now get the hell out of my office."

Chapter XXXIX

UT2 John I. Peffley, whose nickname was P-Fly, could do almost anything; fix plumbing, cook, grow vegetables, build relationships with the locals etc. But he could also pull stunts that gave his boss a red face from time to time.

Being an army officer he probably expected me to salute. Being a navy officer, inside and uncovered, I merely turned around and left. That probably pissed the major off even more.

At any rate I trudged back to the Seabee compound totally in a daze. I was well aware that we had obviously done something we should not have done but I had no earthly idea what it was. My team chief, EOC Corzette, drove in about that time and I told him what I had just experienced, and asked what in the world the major could be talking about. Like Chief Petty Officers throughout the Navy, Chief Corzette, already knew the background on the incident and he gave me a big smile and said, "Get in the jeep Mr. Olsen and let's take a ride. I think I can clear this up right away."

He drove me down to the river where P-Fly was working with the builders to install sawmill equipment which had been provided to us by USAID. As we approached the sawmill site the little kids in that area ran out to the street, waved, smiled and said to us, "Hello, O.K., fuck MAAG!"

P-Fly had struck again!

Chapter XL

Ringnes Beer

IN THE EARLY 80's there was a CNO requirement that all commanding officers conduct "Captain's Calls" intermittently within their units. The audience was to be of a limited number, apparently to insure more free give and take between the sailors and their skipper. In the case of my Seabee battalion the main body was divided into non-rates, petty officers and chiefs for these sessions. The officers had to fend for themselves but they had ample opportunity to raise questions, express concerns and bitch at our regular wardroom mess meetings.

Supposedly the Captain's Calls were established to allow any and all members of a command to ask questions pertaining to the unit and get an immediate response from the "head shed" without having to see their squad leader, the chaplain or submit a special request chit. From the officer and CPO viewpoint it was an exercise designed to circumvent the chain-of-command. But all in all it probably was a worthwhile exercise. It did provide an opportunity to talk, more or less, on a one to one basis with many members of the battalion. It gave me the opportunity to get a first hand assessment of current battalion scuttlebutt as well as to defuse some obvious rumors. It also provided me a chance to pass on to the troops some of my scuttlebutt. This involved comments I had accumulated from COMCBLANT on items of interest to my Seabees. Topics such as potential construction projects, special training, possible future deployment sites, etc. I always tried to emphasize that these were subjects under consideration by the folks in

Little Creek, Va. (the HQ for COMCBLANT) and not yet firmed up. But I suspect they got expanded beyond belief in the EM club and Chiefs mess anyhow. Never the less I made it a point to conduct Captain's calls frequently and after a while I even began to look forward to them.

While my battalion was deployed to Roosevelt Roads in Puerto Rico I had detachments at Diego Garcia in the Indian Ocean as well as Gitmo (Guantanamo Bay), Cuba, Vieques Island, Andros Island and Argentia, Newfoundland. I made it a point to visit my detachments at least once or twice during the deployment, if at all possible. My Master Chief and I would always travel together to the det. deployment site and spend a day or two talking with the troops, meeting the base C.O. and looking at the work underway. In addition to getting a firsthand look at the troops and their morale we could assess the quality of their work. The monthly detachment ops report to the battalion usually said their work was of excellent quality. And generally, it was. But now and again the Master Chief and I pointed out areas where improvement was possible, and required.

But more than anything else we wanted the det. personnel to know firsthand that the command was aware that they still existed and we were concerned about them.

Sometime during the summer of '81 the Master Chief, John Huff and I set up a visit to my detachment in Gitmo. On this occasion we were able to get the station plane to fly us over and back. This was a real treat compared to bumming a ride or some other Navy scheduled flight or even traveling via commercial airlines. The Master Chief and I felt like a couple of Fleet Admirals as we were being flown around in "our" own plane, at our direction, for two days. As a pair of Seabees who were normally happy to have a jeep at their disposal, we were in "tall cotton!"

Upon our arrival in Gitmo the detachment OIC met us and we paid a courtesy call on the base C.O. Following that we had scheduled a quick tour of the job sites. As usual I had the OIC set up an early "knock off" from work that day so I could hold a Captain's call with all of the det. personnel.

My normal practice at detachment sites was to buy a couple cases of beer and have them chilled and ready for the det. Seabees when they came in from work and then hold the Captain's call. I have heard that there are Seabees who don't drink beer but I have to admit I've never met one. But then I only spent 30 years on active duty. In any case the cold beer was always well received. I'm quick to point out this practice did not apply to the 600 man main body. Following the call on the base

Chapter XL

C.O. the OIC drove us over to the Gitmo package store so I could purchase the beer.

Being a U.S. base in a communist county does have a few advantages. For one, there were no taxes. Consequently beer and liquor prices were pretty cheap. And the range of different brands of beers, literally from around the world, was extensive. Beers from the U.S., Europe, Great Britain, Japan, Mexico and even Red Stripe from Jamaica were on their shelves. But what really caught my eye was a display of cases of Ringnes beer from Norway on a pallet right in the middle of the store. And the price was especially attractive. Having been assigned to Norway for two years with NATO I was quite familiar with Ringnes beer. It was, and still is, one of the premier beers in the country. Even after my return to the U.S. and assignment to JCS I once in awhile would splurge and drive into the District to Central Liquor and treat myself to a case of Ringnes. The premium beer (imported) also had a premium price at that time. But now I was being given the opportunity to buy Ringnes at literally bargain basement prices. I quickly told my Master Chief to load up a couple of cases and arrange to have them chilled, while I went to settle up with the cashier.

When I went to pay the cashier told me the posted price of the display was incorrect. In a sense I was not too surprised as it seemed exceedingly low to me when I first read it. So I assumed the worst and wondered what the actual amount might be. I figured even if I had to pay double the listed price it would still be worth it, as Ringnes is a mighty fine beer. But that was not to be. The cashier told me the actual price was actually about half the posted price! I was flabbergasted. Things could not get much better than this. I asked if she was sure of the price and she answered "yup". This was a really fortunate turn of events. The Olsen luck could not get much better. At this point I probably should have suspected something was amiss, but I didn't want to spoil a good thing so I paid quickly and left the package store thinking I'd better get out before the cashier realized she had made an error on the pricing.

The Master Chief and I spent the rest of the day riding around with the detachment OIC looking at the work in progress on the various projects which were scattered around the base at Gitmo. About 1600 (4:00 p.m.) we arrived back at the det. shop spaces to get ready for my Captain's call. The Seabees got to knock off early that day and they soon began to congregate, coming in from all the various job sites. The OIC, John Brandt, opened three beers for the Master Chief, me and himself and we started the "happy hour." The beer was ice cold — but that was its' only redeeming feature. It was flat, had a terrible taste, something between GO-90 and five year old turpentine, as well as a horrible after taste. It's my guess those cases of Ringnes were probably delivered in 1958. That's about the time Castro took over Cuba and the U.S. broke diplomatic relations between Guantanamo and Cuba. The beer had apparently been stored in the back of a warm warehouse for two dozen years or so before it had been put on sale at the package store. In any case the cut rate price I paid in the package store was grossly excessive. Looking back on things I figure they should have paid me just to get rid of some of their overage beer supply.

As I looked at my Master Chief and the OIC I observed a "What the hell is this stuff?" look on their faces.

Before I could say anything Master Chief Huff said, "Don't worry about it Captain." I glanced around the room and watched the Seabees opening and drinking the beers like they were going out of style. As I watched the Ringnes was disappearing quickly. In no time at all both cases were gone.

It only goes to prove that if it is free, wet and cold Seabees will drink it!

Chapter XLI

Greens

BEFORE THE ADVENT OF the camouflage, or battle dress uniform, used by practically all services and all nations these days, the Seabee working uniform was the utility green uniform. Essentially the same working uniform was used by the other services. But in earlier days there were severe restrictions on when and where Seabees could wear that working uniform. It was quite unlike the practice seen today where practically all military personnel can wear their "cammies" everywhere; on base, off base, anywhere in the community even travel in them.

During the period of the '60's and '70's there was no off base travel in greens other than direct home to work travel in a vehicle. Even the on base wear often included some rigid restrictions relative to the wearing of greens. For example there was absolutely no wearing of greens in any of the clubs after 1630.

For the benefit of today's troops I need to explain that there used to be enlisted, chiefs and officers clubs aboard Navy bases. These were clubs where each community would gather to relax with shipmates, usually after work or in the evenings, as opposed to today's all hands clubs which no one patronizes.

Greens were never allowed in the base movie theatre and sometimes were not permitted in the exchange after secure — 1630. Now a days they seem to be acceptable anywhere, anytime. There were a few exceptions for the clubs on various bases in that they sometimes had a "green hour" at the bar after work. To be honest the green hour frequently evolved into green hours as the closing time was generally a nebulous hour. There were some bases that even had a greens bar at specified times or on specific days.

That was the case at Davisville, R.I. in the early 70's. CBC Davisville and NAS Quonset Point were adjacent bases behind the same fence line. The two bases did not have much in common as far as operational units, equipment or missions were concerned, but they did share some facilities together, e.g. hospital, commissary, exchange, BOQ and officers club. The O club never had a greens hour but they did operate a satellite bar in the BOQ which allowed patrons to wear greens and flight suits. Another nice feature of the BOQ bar was that it was open on Mondays while the O club was normally closed.

Consequently Lt. John Milkintas, CWO4 Marty Shelton and I began to meet at the BOQ bar on Mondays after work for our own happy hour. For some reason no other CBC or battalion officers ever showed up at our regular Monday functions. Perhaps they did not want to associate with the airdales. Who knows? But it did not bother the three of us. No matter how many aviators showed up the three of us figured we had them outnumbered and surrounded anyhow. In any case there seldom were pilots who showed up on Mondays. We frequently had the bar to ourselves except for two other regulars; an airdale warrant officer and a nurse.

One particular Monday the three of us were enjoying our brews after work when a group of rowdy airdales came barging into our bar. All of them were pilots except for one who was a NFO. For the uninitiated a NFO or Navy Flight Officer is a non-pilot who flies as a navigator, bombardier, weapons officer or some such duty but he does not drive the aircraft. All of these airdales were wearing the aviation greens uniform which looks a lot like a Marine green uniform in both cut and color. It is a good looking and practical winter working uniform for officers. I have thought for years that the CEC should adopt it as a winter working uniform, especially when working on construction projects.

Back to my story.

For some reason the NFO seemed to have a big mouth and he kept making snide remarks about Seabees who took up space at "their" bar and drank all of "their" booze and also looked like a bunch of plumbers. All three comments were probably accurate. We, of course, pointed out that the airdales would not be able to operate if it were not for the work of the Seabees who built their facilities, runways, etc. Even so the NFO kept on the attack.

Chapter XLI

Finally I backed off from the bar, faced him and said, "You ought not to be treating us so nasty, after all we have a lot in common."

He cocked his head and replied in a doubting manner, "Oh yeah, how's that?"

I said, "Well just look at us, we are both Lieutenant Commanders, we both wear greens and they won't let either one of us drive an airplane."

If he had wanted to make a reply it would not have been heard over the laughter of his pilot buddies.

Chapter XLII

The Marines Ain't So Bad

IN SEPTEMBER OF 1994 the United States sent a military task force ashore on the Caribbean Nation of Haiti, to depose the military junta that had taken control of the country and forced the elected leaders to flee. This was essentially a repeat of what the United States had done 75 years earlier. At that time the Marines were sent to Haiti to oppose a corrupt government that was on the verge of destabilizing a nation on the doorstep of the U.S.A.

By this time I was retired from the Navy and working in the International Division of a U.S. Construction Company. A good portion of our work at that time was for LantDiv (The Atlantic Division of Naval Facilities Engineering Command). Some of our work involved emergency construction, whenever and wherever LantDiv wanted expedient construction services of any nature. Frequently we were called on to provide construction expertise in response to natural disasters, but we were also on call for any unplanned developments, such as invading Haiti. The Army was designated as the onsite commander of all U.S. forces in-country but LantDiv had been tasked to provide support for construction and construction management.

In our particular case we had been requested to survey a project for the Department of Justice (DOJ), specifically to construct a facilities complex for the National Police Training Academy. Two of us flew from New York to Port Au Prince to spend two weeks looking at the job, searching for potential subcontractors as well as developing

Chapter XLII

estimates for the work. To make a long story short, we got back home eight months later. I began to think I was back in the Seabees with deployment extensions such as that.

But that's another story.

As mentioned the Army was in charge of all U.S. Forces and later also some small detachments of other nations U.N. Forces. The Army Commander instituted a set of rigorous controls and guidelines for all troops, including minimal association with the locals, no frequenting of business establishments — particularly bars and restaurants — and no drinking of alcoholic beverages at any time. This last dictum was pretty questionable as Haiti was not a muslim country and adult beverages were available.

Being a civilian contractor we were not subject to all of the Army's restrictions, which was fortunate as it would have been next to impossible to convince a crew of construction stiffs not to have a drink, especially when the drinks were readily available. After all, Haiti is a pretty warm place and a cold beer at the end of the work day is not only enjoyable but practically essential if we were to keep the crew on the job. As it turned out we were not the only ones with that attitude. In restaurants in Petionville, a more or less upper class district of Port Au Prince, we saw the Army Major General who was the troop commander, together with some of his staff, having dinner and drinks on more than one occasion. Apparently this was a case of do as I say, not do as I do. Or perhaps it was a RHIP (rank has its privileges) situation. In any case it was a pretty sorry display of leadership to my way of thinking.

As things turned out we ended up working for DOJ and dealing with one of their contract administrators, and had no direct dealing with the Army. Never the less our work in Haiti often led to other minor construction projects in support of the U.S. troops in the country. Even though the Army was in charge, their construction effort had a CEC Lieutenant Commander running things. Actually LantDiv was in charge of all troop related construction. This was pretty much a hip-pocket operation. It consisted of the LCdr, two Seabee Senior Chiefs, one a builder and the other a steelworker and two pickup trucks.

Being the only U.S. contractor with ongoing operations in Haiti we were asked to quote on several of their minor construction contracts, most of which were $25,000.00 or less. We quickly developed a good working relationship with the three Seabees as we visited their office frequently. The office in question was in the Army command center in a very large warehouse building. It consisted of a laptop computer, two desks, a table, some folding chairs and one big floor mounted pedestal base fan. Being Seabees I suspect the fan was the result of some cumshaw by the Senior Chiefs. Once in awhile they would drive out to our "villa" to use the term loosely, and made use of our swimming pool. They also managed to find time to have a cold beer or two. It was understood that this was not in accordance with Army guidelines, but hey, if it is good enough for the General it ought to be good enough for the troops.

Some folks may think the free beer and dip in the pool constitute a bribe, or gratuity. No way! The Seabees came to us to solicit a quote on their work. We did not seek it out. And to a large measure we did the work as a favor to them. They frequently were unable to find a suitable/qualified/reliable contractor for the type of construction they wanted done. Many times, we had to pull workers from our main job in order to accomplish their work. And besides, we had a better profit margin on the DOJ work than we did on the NavFac work.

At any rate all three of the LantDiv Seabees were pretty perplexed and frustrated with the way the Army ran things. This included their burdensome requirements relative to contracting and construction as well as their double standard on individual conduct. The Senior Chiefs particularly bitched about the Army continually and at varying degrees of intensity. Up until this time I never fully realized just how deep seated this resentment had become. In early '95 when I was visiting the LantDiv office the senior chief steelworker came in and sat next to me. He had another recent Army notice in his hand and a really "hang-dog" expression on his face. Finally he spoke up and put everything in perspective when he said to me, "Captain, after serving with the Army for nearly three months, I take back damn near everything I ever said about the Marine Corps!"

Chapter XLIII

Air Medals

THE NAVY AND MARINE CORPS have always been frugal and parsimonious when it comes to awarding medals to individuals, both the meritorious and heroic awards. That policy seems to have slacked off somewhat these days with the end of tour awards seeming to copy the Army and Air Force practice and becoming almost automatic. This was not always the case however. There are rumors about Marine Corps awards being too generous at times, but a large portion of their awards have been posthumous, which is not the way one likes to be recognized. Like many others who experienced the period covering the Korean and Viet Nam conflicts, I saw many instances of award recommendations being downgraded or completely turned down. One Rear Admiral in the CEC, who had minimum personal awards himself, seemed to have a goal of denying any award recommendation. Apparently he wanted to make sure no one on active duty had more medals than he did. In any case the Navy seemed to be quite stingy in their award approvals. Some of it was perhaps due to poor write ups and justification but all in all the philosophy seemed to be, "Nice job but that's what you were paid to do." Or "A letter of commendation will suffice." During my early battalion tours I continually noticed that the highest personal award most Chief Petty Officers held was the Good Conduct Medal. This was often still the case when they reached retirement. It is pretty discouraging to think that after 20-30 years of military service the most significant thing a fellow has done was to behave himself. In practically all cases that was not the case but for whatever reason the outstanding work or achievement of many individuals was not officially recognized.

About half way through the Viet Nam years the Navy attitude toward awards seemed to become less rigid and more personal decorations began to be presented. This was about the 1967-1968 time frame. Prior to that the only awards that were commonplace were Purple Heart medals. The close association with the Army and their MAAG (Military Assistance Advisory Group) detachments throughout the county may have had some influence on this change in attitude. Where ever you were assigned in South Viet Nam there was a MAAG detachment or detachments somewhere in the province.

In 1964 in Quang Tri province the MAAG detachment was adjacent to our Seabee team compound back fence. At the time my Seabee Team, 0904, was deployed to the northernmost province in the country. The Army unit was continually inviting me to their award presentation ceremonies. After the first one or two I usually declined as we had work to do. But it became quickly obvious that there was a fairly rigid protocol for the Army awards. If you were an officer or senior NCO you received the Bronze Star medal when you completed your tour. If you were a snuffy you got the Army Commendation Medal. While we were there the Army had one Capt. who seemed to cause more headaches for the province senior advisor, a Major, than all the rest of the team combined. Scuttlebutt had it that he would booze it up at the local gin mills, refuse to pay his bills, a couple of times got pretty rowdy and busted up bar furniture, wrecked a jeep, and even tried to get out of paying the local Vietnamese hookers after enjoying their delights. (They should have insisted on payment up front) In any case I learned that when he transferred at the end of his tour sure enough he received a Bronze Star. I guess as long as the various escapades did not escalate to an international incident everything was o.k.

During that time frame the only automatic award given to members of Seabee teams deployed to Viet Nam was the Armed Forces Expeditionary medal. That wasn't so bad and any medal was appreciated by the Seabees. For years we had been accustomed to the policy that the reward for good performance was no punishment, so we were tickled pink to get any medal.

Being in the northernmost province of South Viet Nam we were pretty much on the end of the line logistically and we frequently had to expend considerable effort ourselves in order to insure the items we needed

Chapter XLIII

actually made it to us. This included chow ordered from the Navy commissary in Saigon as well as repair parts for our equipment, fuel from Hue or DaNang and even much of our construction consumables. As a result I frequently sent one or two of my petty officers to the Marine chopper squadron in DaNang or the MAAG sector HQ for I Corps in Hue to locate items we were told had been shipped and to escort them on to our camp site. Traveling was made a lot easier by using the Army's log flights. This usually consisted of a single engine "otter" light plane that could carry 8-10 passengers and/or cargo. For heavy lifts we had to resort to the Air Force in DaNang and plead with them to lay on a C-123 to fly directly to Dong Ha which was only about six or seven miles away.

But the otter was pretty much our main resupply source. It was slow and ugly but it was a super reliable airplane and could take off and land most anywhere. This was both a positive and a negative factor as far as I was concerned. Since the otter could land most anywhere it was used to resupply every outpost the Army had in our province as well as Tua Thien, Hue's province. As a result it frequently took the better part of a day to fly from Quang Tri to DaNang. Starting from Quang-Tri the route went to Dong Ha, Cam Lo, Khe Sanh, Ba Long, Hue Citadel, Hue Phu Bai and then to DaNang. After arrival in DaNang it wasn't uncommon to spend two or three days chasing down our goods and arranging for the return flight to Quang Tri. As a result whoever made the trip could be gone from three to five days. But it also provided my courier the opportunity to enjoy the delights of the big city — DaNang — for a brief period so I thought that was worthwhile.

But what's all this got to do with the awarding of medals? I was just getting to that. Shortly after I redeployed my Seabee team from the hills south of Hue to Quang Tri I took the log flight back to DaNang. I had to resolve personal property records with the Special Forces "C" team for all the items we had left at their "A" team site at Nam Dong when we departed. And besides I wanted to spend some time at the Marine "Shu-Fly" detachment at DaNang. Seabees always felt more comfortable with Marines, not to mention the fact that I needed to replenish my supply of Tabacalera cigars which the Marines imported from the Cubi Point on their resupply flights.

As usual the log flight departed Quang Tri and began the hop scotch route through all the detachment sites on its' way to DaNang. After the first couple of stops I noticed an Army NCO sitting next to me making notations after every take off and landing. I asked why he was doing that. He responded, "It's for my air medal." That didn't sound reasonable to me and I reminded him that he wasn't part of the flight crew so I didn't see how he could qualify for any such award. The sergeant said any flight in a combat zone made him eligible. And furthermore every take off and landing constituted a flight. As a result the trip from Quang Tri to DaNang would provide him with seven flights and another seven on the return trip. He suggested I track the flights as well and put in for the award as something like 25 flights made one eligible. I got to thinking that was only two round trips. With the frequency I was having to send folks to DaNang and Hue everyone on my team could have an air medal by the time we finished our deployment. Naturally I began to note the flying times and airfield locations too.

Still I wasn't convinced the sergeant was all that accurate so I made it a point to talk to the province senior advisor when I returned. He pointed out to me that the air medal was the same award for all the services. And yes, after 25 flights in a combat area any military personnel were eligible for the award. I would have to certify the flights for my Seabees but the Major would be happy to obtain and award the medals. This was good news. Now my Seabees would have at least one personal award apiece after our tour.

I went back to the team house and talked things over with my chief. Since I kept the team log I could make entries there regarding individual flights; dates, locations, etc. All the Seabees would have to do was record their flight times. We talked about the subject that evening and even though some team members were a bit reluctant to fly on the otter if they didn't absolutely have to, everyone seemed to be in favor of making the trips if they could earn a medal. Granted it wasn't a lot to do to become eligible but if that was the way the system worked we might as well take advantage of what was available. To be honest I really wanted to dazzle the rest of the battalion when my guys showed up the next parade wearing air medals.

Just a few days later the OIC for all the Seabee teams' in-country, LCdr. Jack Wright, flew up from Saigon to see how we were getting along. I took him around to meet the province chief, province senior advisor, USAID rep, etc. and also toured our job sites and camp. He seemed to be fairly well pleased with how we had settled in and started our construction program so rapidly. After evening chow we were drinking a beer and talking about nothing in particular when I happened to mention to him that I was working on getting air medals for all of my team. Jack raised his eyebrows and said, "You what?" I was quick to explain how the Army folks had informed us of our eligibility for the medal after 25 individual

Chapter XLIII

flights and with my continuing need to send team members to DaNang; they could easily accumulate the needed number of flights. Jacks expression never changed, he just looked at me and said, "Forget that. You ain't getting any damned Army medals."

Maybe if I had kept my mouth shut we could all have gone back to Port Hueneme looking like heroes. On the other hand someone was bound to have said, "Those are Army medals."

Chapter XLIV

Torremolinos

I ASSUMED COMMAND OF NMCB-74 on 3 July 1980 in Rota, Spain. At that point the deployment was well underway. We had numerous detachment sites throughout the Med, Europe and Diego Garcia as well as a hefty main body workload right there in Rota. All in all the work was going well everywhere. At least that's what I was told during the in-brief. But as the new skipper I wanted to get a look at things myself, both at the detachment sites and throughout the main body.

The line companies work-in-place rate was good and the quality of their work was excellent. My supply officer, LCdr Don Dickey had all aspects of his operation well in hand. Our medical and dental departments always seemed to be busy but fortunately with what seemed to be minor treatment needs. In fact one of their most time consuming functions in those days seemed to be overseeing the pee-in-the-bottle drug screening program.

My battalion master chief, actually senior chief builder Tom Linenberger, took me on a tour of our detachment sites. Tom was an outstanding chief who later became an LDO (limited duty officer). He also had one additional special qualification not often found in sailors. Like me, he was also from Kansas. But I digress. Most everything at our det. sites was also in good shape and the host station C.O.'s gave me glowing endorsements of my Seabees.

Unlike some of the '60's deployment sites, each location had a wide range of options for the Seabees off duty hours. In addition to the "slop chute" (EM club) there was a town nearby, sports activities such as basketball, baseball and flag football, etc. were available. Also each shore station was staffed with a number of "soft sailors" which always made life more enjoyable. Well all right — I will confess Diego Garcia was still lacking some of those amenities.

At the main body site in Rota we had one other valuable asset to support our R&R program. A bus. Being a deployed outfit we were not allowed to have private vehicles. But CBLANT did arrange for us to have a nice "over the road" type of bus — as opposed to a school bus — for the troops to use for week end R&R travel, in comfort, for trips to various locations. This was a new wrinkle to me but something I was pleased to see. As a junior officer in a Pacific battalion I was used to deployments to Midway and Adak. The only liberty there was strolling around the Navy Exchange or walks on the beach. Unfortunately that was still the situation for my troops on Diego Garcia. But our location near the Mediterranean Sea offered us many options for day trips and even some week-end trips. We owned the bus and provided our own driver so we could do whatever we wanted relative to scheduling travel. It was a great opportunity for the troops. I wanted to make sure we made maximum use of this valuable asset.

A first class builder, BU1 Tom Stark, was in charge of our special services program and he ran things quite well. He coordinated with the base special services folks on activities and managed to keep the Seabees informed of what was available on base. He was also very active in organizing our sports teams; baseball, basketball and even the tackle football teams in the fall and he made sure we had a slot on the various sports leagues on base. He ran a sports gear locker for the battalion where Seabees could obtain any necessary items for pick-up games. He did a lot of other tasks relative to providing opportunities for off-duty entertainment and he scheduled the liberty bus. At the time that was my concern.

I asked about the various destinations the bus traveled to on their liberty runs and was surprised when I was told they only went to Torremolinos, which was a beach town about 135 miles away. He said it went every Sunday and was always full. It made sense to me that the Seabees would be attracted to a beach town on the Med. No doubt it was a popular place with lots of girls in bikinis. Of course we had easy access to a beach in Rota but with a big Spanish naval base as well as the U.S. contingent there the competition could be pretty rough. It might well have been easier to meet girls in Torremolinos. Even so, I thought it was still a mistake to ignore the other options. Why not go to Gibralter, it was only 75 miles away. Even though it was British access to the rock was not a problem. Seville was only 75 miles away, it was a historic and beautiful city with lots of attractions. Even a 300 mile trip to Lisbon was possible. Why not offer some different options, I asked.

Stark had sort of a puzzled look on his face but he replied that they had offered trips to other places early in the deployment but no one was interested. They all wanted to go to Torremolinos. Finally I asked, "What's so great about Torremolinos?" Looking back on it now I realize that what I took for a puzzled look was actually an expression of disbelief. Stark was too polite, or intimidated, to say "How dumb can you be?" Instead he just said, "TITS, Captain, TITS".

As it turned out Torremolinos was the nearest nude beach in Spain. Apparently everyone in the battalion except the new skipper was aware of that fact. The Seabees knew what they liked and Torremolinos provided all the "culture" they could handle.

Even battalion commanding officers have to learn a few things the hard way.

Chapter XLV

Merry Christmas

$\mathcal{S}$OMETIMES IT IS SIMPLY amazing the lengths someone will go to or the inconvenience they suffer themselves in order to play a practical joke or someone else. Seabees are certainly no exception to this behavior. I witnessed a vivid demonstration of this in December '63 when the MCB-NINE main body was returning from deployment on Okinawa.

But again, I'm getting a little ahead of myself.

We had completed our deployment in early December and were being relieved, on site, by MCB-FIVE. It was common in those days for the bulk of the battalion to travel to and from the deployment sites by troop ship. As usual, we were going aboard the *USS Mitchell*. For some reason no matter if we were coming or going, or which deployment site in the Pacific we were dealing with, we always seemed to travel aboard the *Mitchell*. This is in spite of the fact that there were several other troop ships in the Pacific fleet. We began to think we knew that ship better than the ships company.

After FIVE disembarked in Okinawa we backfilled their spaces for the return cruise to Port Hueneme. The schedule had us arriving on 22 Dec, just before Christmas. But first we would have to make a run to Korea to drop off the Army troops. Coming out from ConUS the ship carried Seabees and Marines for Okinawa and soldiers for Korea. They took roughly the same number of troops on the return trip back to the U.S. The usual shipboard practice for the cruise was to have the Marines stand the required watches and the Army troops do the mess cooking while the Seabees would perform minor repair work aboard the ship.

This was fine with us as it gave our Seabees something to do, and it provided a way to keep a portion of our troops occupied. The Marines had it easy as there were not many watch stations. Doing all the mess cooking from early morning until late at night was quite demanding so the Army troops were not too happy.

At any rate the main body boarded the ship in Naha on 8 Dec. and we set sail immediately for Incheon, Korea. The total cruise would take about two weeks. To most all of the troops aboard this would be essentially two weeks with pay. There would be little or no duty or in any case not what one would call rigorous duty. After a busy nine month deployment, which included a good many hours of extra duty we all figured we had earned a few days to "kick back."

When we arrived at Incheon to swap out the Army troops the weather was terrible. Cold, windy, blowing rain — nearly sleet. Due to the extreme tidal range at Incheon the ship had to anchor out and transfer the troops to shore using Mike boats. Once the ship was in position the harbor master brought out a pontoon string which was tied up to the ship with the pontoons perpendicular to the ship. The outboard end of the pontoon string was an ell and there was an angled ramp into the water just inboard of the ell. The Mike boat would tie up inboard of the ell and lower the bow ramp to discharge and receive the passengers.

The transfer procedure most likely worked quite well when the weather was decent. But it was a miserable exercise in a storm. Following the usual military practice of "hurry up and wait" the troops going to Korea were staged on the pontoons with their duffle bags and getting thoroughly drenched while waiting for the Mike boat to come out. When it reached the pontoons the troops going home would offload and then the arriving troops would board and make their way into shore, getting wetter and colder all the while. Not an enjoyable exercise for anybody involved.

The Incheon troop swap had just gotten underway when a pair of battalion junior officers, Ralph Neely and Glenn Weaver burst into our stateroom saying, "You got to come see this!"

"See what?"

"You will find out, come on."

I threw on my field jacket, watch cap and gloves and followed them out onto the weather deck. There must have been 15 to 20 Seabees out there huddled under an overhang out of the rain. But still it was pretty cold and uncomfortable. There was really no cause for them to be out in such

Chapter XLV

weather. Even though they were somewhat sheltered from the rain they still had to endure the wind and cold. I asked myself why in the world are they out here?

The quick answer was they were watching the Army troops. But why?

After the Mike boat discharged the homeward bound soldiers and the wet and bedraggled doggies boarded, the Mike boat would raise the bow ramp and back away from the pontoons. Once clear of the pontoons the coxswain would throttle down and shift to a forward gear for the run to the beach.

During this brief period when there was no noise from the engine and all was quiet, one of the Seabees would command, "One, two, three." Then all of the other Seabees present would holler as a group, "Merry Christmas!" Talk about rubbing salt into a wound.

Chapter XLVI

Tabacaleras

I NEVER REALLY BECAME a smoker. When many of my high school friends took up the habit I took a pass on it. Part of my reasoning was that I knew it was not good for you from a health standpoint. The coach said it diminished your wind, or some such logic. And I wasn't that much of an athlete in the first place so I did not want to add to my limitations. The second reason was probably more profound. I was too cheap to buy cigarettes and have my buddies bum them off me as they always seemed to be doing with each other. Whatever the case I did not get around to becoming a smoker.

Years later I did smoke a cigar now and then. Whenever a new father passed them out to celebrate the birth of a son or daughter, or any other significant event. And there were a couple periods when I was overseas that I smoked cigars on a more or less regular basis. This happened during my first Seabee team tour in Viet Nam in 1964.

We deployed to Thua Thien and Quang Tri, the two northernmost provinces in South Viet Nam. The team consisted of one officer, one chief, one corpsman and ten Seabee ratings. There was no allowance for support troops so I handled most all of the admin work. Early on I developed a routine that seemed to work well. Everybody on the team was usually out working on projects during the day. Following the evening meal I would light my cigar and proceed to write up the teams activities for the day in our log. Not exactly an exciting event but

Chapter XLVI

frequently it was the highlight of the day. And the cigar — it kept the mosquitoes away.

Tobacco products are pretty much available around the world and Viet Nam was no exception. Many remnants of the French influence throughout Indo China were positive. Good bread, wine and nice eating places were some of the positive carry overs. On the other hand tobacco products were some of the most potent you can imagine. But that was not a problem as I had an alternative. For some time a Marine helicopter detachment had been operating out of the air field at Da Nang and they kept themselves stocked with beer and cigars from the Philippines via their weekly resupply flights.

Although we were roughly 90 miles north of Da Nang there seemed to be a frequent requirement for one of the team members to take a trip there for one reason or another. I always made sure they would come back with a box of Tabacalera cigars from the Marine canteen. Even though it seemed to be a hap hazard resupply method I don't ever recall running out of cigars.

The Philippine Tabacalera cigars come in numerous varieties but the one most popular with the Marine aviators, and me, was about seven inches long and about ¾ inch in diameter and smooth and mild. Being the preferred cigar of the Marines insured that there would always be ample supply available. But puffing on a cigar during my evening chores was not the only benefit I enjoyed as a result of my tobacco vice. I don't recall exactly when it became apparent but sometime after we redeployed to Quang Tri I began to realize that a cigar, particularly a big long imported cigar, was an object of desire and a status symbol among the locals.

This came about initially by virtue of our working with some ARVN dump truck drivers. One of our earliest projects in Quang Tri province was a road building job. This involved moving a considerable volume of laterite from a pit west of town quite some distance to our project site. Our hauling capability consisted of one 5 ton dump truck. But there was an ARVN engineer outfit in Hue with a number of two and a half ton dump trucks, with drivers. With the help of Danny Whitfield, the province USOM rep, we managed to get four trucks and drivers assigned to us for the project which was several weeks duration. Since the drivers were based in Hue I had to agree to let them return home one day every week. Our dump truck crew would drive up from Hue on Sunday afternoon or Monday morning and work all week until quitting time on Saturday, about 1700 (5:00 p.m.) Then they would drive back to Hue for a short weekend at home. Before leaving for their drive south the lead driver, we called him Barney Oldfield due to his fast driving habits, would come to see me to let me know they were departing. This could have been simply military courtesy but more likely it was to collect their "gratuity." They were of course paid by the ARVN with no remuneration from the team or the province. But from the first week I made it a practice to give each driver one of my Tabacalera cigars. Initially they all mounted the trucks, lit their cigars and began rolling south, puffing up a storm. Later they would accept the cigars and either smoked them after getting to Hue, where they could impress others, or perhaps swapped them for something. In any case they really appreciated the cigars and did not want to miss out on receiving one each week. One Saturday I was tied up somewhere in the afternoon, probably with the province or USAID people, and did not get back to the team house until about 1800. The drivers were still there so I quickly dispensed the cigars so they could get moving. I seem to recall giving them each two cigars that time.

Another cigar incident involved the RF/PF guard squad which provided security around some of our project sites. The RF/PF stands for regional forces/province forces. They were a sort of National Guard unit for the province and we had a squad of them assigned to my team. We uncharitably referred to them as the "ruff and puffs." While they were with the team they lived in a squad tent in our compound.

At this point the exact details of the event are a little hazy but essentially what happened was that the RF/PF crew somehow routed out a VC who was scoping out our operation at the laterite pit. Keep in mind this occurred after we had already been ambushed once by the VC at that site so we were a bit concerned with anyone who was not a villager. The RF/PF troops took the guy into custody and delivered him to the province military in Quang Tri, who quickly established that he was in fact a VC and most likely involved in gathering info on the site for another attack.

According to my chief the province military took custody of the V.C. and more or less just dismissed the RF/PF troops without even so much as a "thank you" or "well done." The chief and I quickly decided that they deserved some sort of recognition for their actions. After going through one ambush at that site we were quite appreciative of the fact that we had apparently avoided a second by virtue of the efforts of the ruff and puffs. That evening after we secured from work I congratulated the squad for their diligence and military actions and then we opened up our team beer cooler. I also gave each squad member a cigar. The beer was appreciated but not all that unique as a good local beer ba mui ba, or 33, was always

Chapter XLVI

The local guard platoon celebrating their capture of a VC with free beer from the team. This was before I had distributed the celebratory cigars.

available somewhere. But a cigar was something else again. They were puffing cigars, blowing smoke in each other's faces, holding their cigars at arm's length to tap off the ash and all sorts of show off actions. I'm convinced they thought more of receiving those cigars than if they had been awarded the Viet Namese Medal of Honor (3rd class)

Another cigar recipient was Papa-San. He was an older Viet Namese man that we inherited from the team we relieved. It was difficult to tell how old he really was. Maybe 50's or 60's or even in his 70's. Who knows? But he for sure had seen many summers. Like most Vietnamese he was quite skinny, what hair he had left was all grey, he was missing a good many teeth but never the less he was always smiling. He was originally hired to be a sort of compound watchman during the day when the team members were out working on projects. That certainly made sense. Even though we did not feel that we had much that was worth stealing the locals looked at it differently. Consequently it was a prudent move to have someone around at all times to make sure the curiosity seekers, as well as the thieves, kept their distance. Even if the mechanics were in the compound working on our equipment they could not keep an eye on everything. And there were times when even the mechanics were out working on a project. Papa-san quickly developed a proprietary interest in all things Seabee as well as our equipment and supplies and everything within our compound. He was a superb watchman.

Sometime later I got the word that the team was being moved to Quang Tri. Even though his family lived in Hue Papa-san indicated he wanted to move with us. That was fine with me but he would now be living with the team and unable to see his family. To get around this problem we agreed that he would get one two day week end each month when he could return to Hue.

Like many Vietnamese Papa-san was a catholic. In Quang Tri, the province capital, the catholic church had a large basilica not far from our team house. Naturally he made it a point to attend regularly. His Sunday "go to meeting" clothes were quite a departure from his normal work day outfit which consisted of flip-flops, shorts and tee shirt. On Sundays he wore shoes and socks, long pants, a shirt with a collar, a white cotton jacket much like a bus boy might wear and a black beret. The beret had an embroidered Seabee patch sewn onto the front panel. Obviously Papa-san cut a pretty wide swath when he went to town. On Sundays the team did not normally do any project work but we stayed in the compound and did maintenance work on equipment or other chores around the house until noon. Our Sunday afternoons were free time. We usually spent the afternoon reading, writing letters, sightseeing around town and making ice cream with a hand crank freezer I brought along. Meanwhile Papa-san would get togged out in his church gear and about mid morning he would come to see me to let me know he was on his way to church. That was when I gave him his weekly cigar. But he would not smoke it right away. Apparently he took it with him to church and lit it up after the service as he normally showed up back at the team house shortly after noon still puffing his cigar.

Later on he would collect all the weekly cigars and hoard them until he made his monthly trip back home to Hue. About noon time on Saturday he would put on his "Sunday best," pack his ditty bag, actually someone's cast off AWOL bag, go over the highway across from the team house, set down his bag, light a cigar and wait for the bus. Compared to the usual majority of passengers; old ladies, kids, pigs, etc. Papa-san stood out like a celebrity. And he always seemed to get one of the special seats in the front of the bus. I don't know if it was how he was dressed, or the cigar, or a combination of the two but in any case it appeared that he traveled in first class. Or as close as one could come to first class on a provincial bus line.

Chapter XLVI

Considering my largesse with the cigars as rewards/bribes, etc. and the frequency with which they were passed out, I probably did not smoke half of those I bought. In any case it was money well spent.

Chapter XLVII

Wardroom Dinners

*W*HEN I WAS A junior officer on Okinawa wardroom messes were commonplace and expected in all battalions. Admittedly that was when we still had steward's mates in the Navy so the means to operate a wardroom was much easier in those days. Even so, the stewards were primarily responsible for preparing and serving the food. The bar was an officer requirement entirely. And the wardroom bar was the center of activity for the battalion officers and guests as well as the principal money maker for the mess. The mess caterer and the mess treasurer, both officers, handled the supplies and finances but it was our bar girl, Shigeko, who made sure the beer was cold, the popcorn popped and all the drink chits signed. In short she insured that all drinks were paid for. Once in awhile an officer might spend more time than he should in the bar and as the evening progressed he might order a drink and forget to sign a drink chit. These were kept on the bar and all one had to do was write your name and note the number of drinks. If you neglected to do this, no problem. Shigeko would do it for you. Booze, beer and cigarettes were unbelievably cheap on Okinawa as it was then a tax free territory administered by the U.S. Army. As a result all drinks; beer, whisky, cognac, coca cola, etc. were ten cents. But even at that nominal price we were making money.

The Seabee wardroom itself was a pretty modest affair. Like most of our camp it consisted of a couple of quonset huts. Not real impressive from either the outside or inside. But the teachers from the

Chapter XLVII

DoD schools at nearby Kadena Air Base liked it. When they showed up and our banjo playing battalion doctor got going the Seabee wardroom was a great place to be. Most of the time these events just seemed to occur. On other occasions we would have a special event to celebrate, such as a teacher's birthday or the skipper would invite other island commanding officers and their wives to the wardroom for dinner. As members of the mess the junior officers were also entitled to invite guests and we did. But our guest list usually only contained the names of the school teachers. All the other services on the island; Army, Navy, Air Force and even a good percentage of the Marines were assigned to Okinawa on what the Navy calls overseas shore duty. Consequently they had their families with them. The Seabees, being a fleet unit, just as a ship, were deployed without dependents. Our skippers invitations for dinner were to some degree political in that he used them to build good relations with other commands on the island, I suppose it worked pretty much that way particularly after he advised the wardroom that Capt. or Col. so-and-so and his wife were coming to dinner on a certain date and that all officers should be on their best behavior. For the most part it worked that way as no one else would invite a guest on those nights. But I recall the skipper only invited the commanding officers of Navy and Marine outfits. Most likely he figured they would be somewhat tolerant of any rowdy junior officer antics.

About two months before the end of our deployment the idea of a big wardroom party developed. And it came off quite well. Special chow that might, a small band and even some na-sans performing traditional Japanese dances. Well maybe it was not all that traditional as they performed the dances with and without clothing. The only guests for this party were the school teachers and they seemed to enjoy the show as much as the officers. When we got to the nude dancing I recall one teacher commenting, "My boobs are bigger than hers!" I don't recall that she offered to prove it however.

As the saying goes: A good time was had by all. But there were repercussions. At least one. The party bankrupted the mess treasury and we had an immediate assessment of something like five or seven dollars per member. That was not so bad but the real kicker came when we raised the drink prices from ten cents to fifteen cents. A fifty percent price boost is pretty substantial but when one considered that the 50% only came out to a nickel we pretty much accepted it and figured it was money well spent. All except one officer who was a tea-totaller. He made the point that he felt he was subsidizing all us boozers. Such was not the case. The mess treasurer quickly pointed out that soft drinks on the island cost more than beer and booze, something like twelve cents a can, so we in effect had been subsidizing him. But now he was going to have to pay his own way.

In any case the officer's wardroom was a vital part of the battalion organization. The officers quickly became indoctrinated as members of "their" battalion, a unit esprit de corps flourished, a tight knit social group emerged and spin-offs such as mission and duty business was conducted informally. But not at the bar as any business talk at the bar was verboten.

Following Viet Nam I drew a series of assignments away from the Seabees for nearly twelve years: schools, public works, staff jobs, etc. But eventually I got orders back to a battalion. This was in 1980. During the interim there had been many changes made throughout DoD and one of the most significant was the elimination of the club system for the military and the implementation of what the Navy called the "all hands club." I have no idea what the rationale was behind this change but if it was to eliminate the military club system it was highly effective. There was no way the officers, chiefs and snuffies were all going to the same bar to socialize after working hours. This may have had some effect on the total alcohol consumption, but I doubt it. On the other hand it may simply have been another cost reduction move by some civilian "whiz-kid" in DoD who was left over from years earlier. Whatever the case it was a big mistake.

In any case when I assumed command of my Seabee battalion in Rota in July '80 I learned immediately that there was no officer's wardroom or mess. The officers were all being paid deployment per diem and paying for each of the meals consumed at the prescribed rate. The chow was all prepared at the main galley and transported to the officers quarters area in large thermos bottles. Needless to say that did not enhance the taste, temperature or appearance of the chow. As a result most all of the junior officers were eating at the station gedunk, out of vending machines or trying to live on a six pack of Dr. Pepper and a bag of Fritos for a week and pocket the difference. I recognized the need for a wardroom mess right away. After a quick meeting with my X.O. and supply officer we concluded that we were essentially a deployed unit and in accordance with Navy regulations and the BuSandA (Bureau of Supplies and Accounts) manual we were essentially an "afloat unit" and eligible to establish our own mess. The next step was to hold an all officers meeting and give them the word on the establishment of the mess. My supply officer, Don Dickey, quickly described how the mess

Chapter XLVII

would operate and how it would be funded by all the members. In effect every member paid in to establish the mess fund and all would pay their share for the month for meals served. Deductions for officers traveling out of the area were allowed and bar bills were extra. Mess bills were to be tendered and paid monthly. Most of the junior officers were quite apprehensive even after the briefing but I received some unexpected support from our battalion chaplain. He was a former WWII boiler tender who had been a fireman in Memphis for over 20 years. After that he went to seminary, was ordained and quickly found himself back in the Navy. He announced to the wardroom that a wardroom mess was commonplace on every ship he had been aboard and if we did not have one we were essentially saying we were not a fleet unit. There was not much further discussion after the chaplain's remarks. I announced the mess would begin in a week or so and the mess treasurer would be around to collect the initial mess payment on payday.

We planned to have hot breakfasts every day, four evening meals — Monday through Thursday. Noon meals and weekend dinners would not be served. This was practical as many officers would be away from the battalion on jobs during the work week and touring around the area on week-ends. It also provided for some time off for our cook. In less than a month's time I had several officers inform me that they were not only eating much better but they were even saving more money than they had previously. They were also getting a much better diet and I was getting a really tight knit wardroom community. Admittedly our supply officer made sure we had one of the best cooks in the battalion so that was one more advantage. After a brief shake down period our cook, a second class, really took to the job. He appreciated the opportunity to develop and exhibit his culinary talents and he would out do himself when we had guests as the mess.

We established Thursday night as our guest night and as expected it quickly became a social event for officers and their wives around the naval station to be invited to the Seabee wardroom. Our first guest was the base C.O. Capt. Render Creighton and his wife. I had become acquainted with him earlier in Norfolk and we both assumed command about the same time. He also had the distinction of being a P.O.W. in Hanoi for several years. Most of my officers invited their base counterparts as well, i.e. the base chaplain, supply officer, doctor, dentist, etc. And of course we immediately extended invitations to the nurses. Actually the nurse invitations were almost automatic as our battalion dentist was dating one of the nurses, so it was a natural progression to invite the entire nurse community and they were eager to accept. It certainly did not hurt to have some attractive Navy nurses at our bar frequently and it also kept most all of my junior officers on base during their off hours.

But it was the wardroom dinners that got most of the attention. They were pretty straight forward events; cocktails, socialize, dinner. No program, no speaker other than to introduce and welcome our guests. I was pleasantly surprised at the "couth" my junior officers could exhibit in mixed company.

Rota is actually a Spanish Naval Base and the U.S. is a tenant even though the American forces ran the larger operation. RAdm Cruz was their senior officer and the Spanish HQ was just across the road from the Seabee camp. I had made my official call on the admiral shortly after arriving in Rota. About three weeks after we established our wardroom mess I felt confident we could entertain properly so I invited Admiral and Mrs. Cruz to dinner. The Admiral was not exactly fluent in English but he was competent. On the other hand my Spanish was nil and Mrs. Cruz knew very little English. I also invited the base Public Works Officer and his wife. Fortunately the Public Works Officer at Rota was Capt. Dan Leonard. He and his wife Vaughan Lea were both practically fluent in Spanish. Besides being an old friend Dan was also a former skipper of my battalion, NMCB-74. Dan was a great sounding board and confidant to me on battalion matters while in Rota. Now he and his wife were coming to my rescue again.

We normally secured at 1630 so we set 1800 as cocktail hour with dinner at 1900. My X.O., Dave Binning and I set the schedule without consulting anyone. After all this was our usual schedule for guest dinners so why should things be any different. Admiral and Mrs. Cruz were very congenial and seemed to enjoy themselves and the dinner. I seem to recall the dinner being especially good as our cook made an extra effort on behalf of the admiral's visit.

After the admiral and most of the other guests had taken their leave I was chatting with Dan and Vaughan Lea when Dan said to me, "I don't suppose you are aware of it but you were doubly honored tonight."

I had to admit I was not aware of anything other than the admiral's presence but I was curious about the two special honors.

Dan said one special distinction was the fact that Mrs. Cruz attended. This was particularly significant because she was known to never attend any U.S. sponsored events, official or social.

I could not think of any response other than to say that's nice, and I asked what the second item was.

Chapter XLVII

Dan gave me a big smile and said; "The admiral ate dinner three hours early!"

Being a newcomer in Spain I was not aware of the usual practice of eating the evening meal around 2200 (10:00 p.m.)

I invited Admiral and Mrs. Cruz over for dinner once more before we redeployed back to our home port in Mississippi.

This time we sort of split the difference; cocktails at 2000, dinner at 2100.

Chapter XLVIII

Østerås

WHEN THE DETAILER tells you that your next duty assignment is to a NATO job, practically all of us are pleased with the news. Granted it is a staff job, which most all engineers detest, but it is a joint staff on a unified command and an international staff at that. Those are all positive elements when promotions are being considered. But when the detailer also says it's the NATO staff in Oslo, I was elated. Norway is my homeland. Things couldn't get any better.

My enthusiasm was dampened somewhat when I began to get into all the preliminary documentation necessary to obtain the NATO clearances as well as to affect the transfer. My official passport had to be renewed and I had to obtain original passports for my children. The next big task was to complete all the forms that were essential back-up for my application for a NATO top secret clearance. I had held a U.S. top secret clearance before so I assumed it would just be renewed. Not so. As the NIS (Navy Intelligence Service) guy explained to me, the U.S. clearance is more or less the gold standard. The NATO clearance is the platinum standard. I guess he was right as I completed numerous forms dealing with my background, references, former supervisors, residence addresses, etc. At the time I thought the info I had provided was extensive and overdone. I was wrong. Sometime later I learned that the NIS folks had even talked with people who were not on any of my listings. I have no idea where or how they obtained those names. Many of them were friends and acquaintances having nothing to do with my education, work or the Navy.

Chapter XLVIII

One of that group had an experience that was rather humorous; at least it was to me but perhaps not for the individual in question. This was a friend of mine in Houston, an architect that I met while going to graduate school at Rice. The NIS guy called at his home during the day and naturally he was at work. His wife was also working but they had a maid who answered the door. The NIS agent told the maid who he was and he wanted to speak with Mr. Newton. Later that afternoon when he returned the maid told "Newt" that a man from the IRS had come to see him but he would be back tomorrow. Needless to say "Newt" had a sleepless night.

Later I learned they had also contacted a lawyer I had used in Nevada and many others who were acquainted with me but were not listed on any information that I had provided. There is no question about it the NIS was extremely thorough in their investigation. Or maybe it was just a slow period for them. In any case several of my friends who were interviewed later told me the main object of their questions had to do with my drinking habits. Apparently DoD was extra cautious when it came to sending anyone with a drinking problem, or even significant drinking habits, to Norway. As I later learned Norway had some of the most stringent drinking and driving laws in Europe, and the Pentagon wanted to forestall any potential problems in that regard.

Eventually I got the screening process completed and I received my orders to Oslo. I arrived there on 10 July '75 and was met at Fornebu, the old Oslo airport on the southwest side of the city adjacent to the fjord, by my new boss. Lt. Col. George Barnes, USAF, had arrived only days earlier. We picked up my gear and went into town where he had arranged a room for me in an old pension near downtown. George said he would send a car for me in the morning, around 0800, to take me to the headquarters so I could check in.

By this time it was mid day and although I did not get much sleep on the flight I was not tired. The excitement of being in Oslo probably kept me energized. In any case I wanted to get out and explore the city. The manager of the pension suggested I walk over to Frogner park which was only a few blocks away. That was a great suggestion. Frogner park, on the west side of central Oslo is filled with human figure sculptures by Gustav Vigeland. They are all nudes, both male and female and all ages, from a fetus to old age and every age in between. There are well over 500 individual statues, friezes and plaques, most of them being multi-figure sculptures. It is a must see attraction for anyone visiting Oslo, at any time of the year.

As mentioned, it was July and the park also operated a beer garden and outdoor cafe during the summer months. A very civilized way to enjoy the season, I thought. After my walking tour of the park I retired to the beer garden. Even though the Norwegian word for beer is øl the waiters had obviously been exposed to numerous utlendinger (foreigners) so they easily understood my request for a beer. In short order the waiter delivered a half liter of Ringnes in a frosty glass. It tasted great. He also delivered a bill which I paid immediately with Norwegian kroner. But it did seem to be a bit expensive to me. At that time I was used to getting change from a dollar when I bought a beer at a bar, even in California. I realized the prices in Norway would be quite a bit higher but even so the amount I had been charged seemed to be pretty steep. I had exchanged some dollars for NKr at the airport but I was not yet accustomed to dealing in kroner. I quickly made a mental calculation of the dollar cost of my beer and it came to about eight dollars! That couldn't be right. So I got my pencil out and using the exchange rate and my tab I recalculated the cost of my beer. Sure enough, it cost over $8 U.S.! Needless to say I only had one beer. This was just the first of several abrupt introductions and adjustments to living in Norway.

Since it had been a relatively short night flying east over six time zones I headed back to the pension. I got my uniform ready for the next day and had some early chow at a nearby restaurant. Also fairly costly but nothing like the beer prices. And I hit the sack early. When I awoke the next morning the sun's rays were beaming through the window and the birds were chirping outside. I had overslept! The car had probably been waiting outside for some time. I gave myself a rapid shave and managed not to nick anything vital, jumped into my uniform, grabbed my paperwork and cover and ran downstairs and out on the street. No sedan was in sight. In fact there was very little traffic either vehicular or pedestrian. I looked at my watch and it said 0315. It must have stopped. I went back inside to the lobby and checked their wall clock. It also registered 0315. Then it dawned on me. This was Oslo in the summer. Even though it was only a quarter after three the sun was already up.

At this point I decided the hell with it, I was not going back to bed so I made myself a cup of coffee and ate several pieces of flat bread for breakfast, attempted to read yesterday's Norwegian newspaper and waited for the car to show up.

The check in at AFNORTH went fairly smoothly. One of my first days on board they conducted an in-brief for all the new arrivals. AFNORTH was basically a British Army HQ consequently they handled most of the

Chapter XLVIII

indoctrination. Then there was the U.S. only in-brief. This consisted principally of a one hour don't drink and drive lecture. In Norway the police could stop a motorist for any or all reasons or even for no reason at all and have the driver blow into a balloon for their preliminary drunk driver field test. If a driver would refuse the balloon test he was automatically guilty. If this was a first offense and there was no accident or traffic laws broken but the balloon changed color the driver was given a significant fine and spent two weeks in the drunk driving jail. This was separate and distinct from the criminal jail. And it was supposedly always full, and had a waiting list of miscreants who had been convicted and needed to serve their jail time.

In the case of U.S. personnel they did not have to ask about the punishment for a second offense as they received a one way ticket back to the U.S. upon their release from jail. The lecturer liked to point out that most everyone would be "legally" drunk for two to three hours after consuming one beer. Obviously happy hours were a thing of the past.

We were all advised to convert immediately to the standard Norsk party procedures. i.e. take a taxi, agree who in the party would be the designated driver and avoid alcohol for the evening or use the bus. Actually the bus was used much more than one might imagine. When there were formal parties at the headquarters, and there were several each year, where the officers wore their mess dress and the ladies were in long gowns, the commandant would send a series of busses around the area to transport everyone to the headquarters and back home after the party. These were available to all officers who did not normally have a car and driver assigned which was about 98 percent of the staff.

As an engineer I was assigned to the infrastructure branch which was part of the logistics operations. As mentioned my immediate boss in infrastructure was a USAF Lt. Col. The next level was a U.S. Army Colonel and the Deputy Chief of Staff for Logistics was a Norwegian Army Major General. I had a personal in-brief with each of them. The most meaningful and the most interesting and unforgettable session was with Major General Sverre "Jimmy" Bratland, Norwegian Army. I have no idea how or when he got the nickname "Jimmy". It is not important since he was addressed as General by all of us. But the wives all called him "Jimmy" as he had requested. He was fairly short, about 5 foot 6 inches, a bit stocky and nearing retirement. He was a much decorated WWII veteran having made the Normandy invasion as a lieutenant, and fought in Europe until VE day. He was a highly regarded general officer in the Norsk forsvarets (Norwegian military forces.) During my travels around the Norwegian bases I met a good many Norwegian general officers and as soon as they learned I was from the NATO HQ in Oslo practically all of them would tell me to pass their respects to Gen. Bratland. Which I was most pleased to do. In a sense one might say he was rather low key but very knowledgeable and quite effective. He also had a subtle sense of humor. When he made a joke or a side comment on a subject in a humorous vein and the person who was the object of the comment finally "got it", he would not laugh out loud but rather smile broadly and sort of chuckle to himself.

My reporting aboard meeting with him was interesting, amusing and illustrates how tolerant he was of us utlendinger. Initially he asked how I was doing in the way of getting settled. That was an early concern for practically everyone assigned to NATO since all but the flag and general officers had to live on the economy. The non-Norwegian general officers apparently had quarters provided by their embassies. But that included only four officers. In my case I rented an apartment in a high-rise condo complex (six stories. In Norway that's a high rise) not far from the headquarters. Gen. Bratland asked where the apartment was located. The area or town was called Østerås. At that point I was not at all familiar with the three extra letters in the Norsk alphabet: Æ, Ø and Å and I sure did not know how to pronounce them. And the word I needed to say contained two of the three. I think I first said OW ster US.

The general said he didn't think he knew where that was. This seemed a bit strange to me as that was where the building was located that housed the U.S. commissary and exchange. Even though Gen. Bratland did not patronize those facilities I was sure he must know where they were. At any rate we continued with our conversation. After a while he asked again the name of the town where my apartment was located. I knew right away that my earlier pronunciation was not correct so this time I pronounced it ER ster OUS. I got the same reaction. This time the general replied that he still could not place that town. Toward the end of our conversation, just before I was to leave he asked once more the name of the town where I would be living. Obviously I had already screwed up the pronunciation twice so I changed it again. This time I said OO ster OHS. General Bratland smiled and said "Oh Østerås, yes, that's where I live."

And he did. He and his wife lived just around the corner from me.

That experience just reinforced my earlier realization that I was no linguist.

Chapter XLIX

Send A Driver

ONE SURPRISINGLY NICE benefit that was part of a NATO assignment was the practice of traveling first class on nearly all official travel. This did not apply to commercial air travel but for all other modes; ship, ferry and rail, the traveler was provided with first class cabin tickets. This might not be as luxurious as some might imagine as most all public transportation in Europe is only of two classes; first and economy, or steerage. But there is usually quite a noticeable difference between the amenities of the two classes. And traveling first class, in Europe, is a definite plus. Considering that most of my travel to the northern naval bases involved rail or ship travel it was a significant perquisite.

And this elite travel status I was able to enjoy was from portal to portal. In other words it began at my front door and continued until I returned home. At every NATO HQ the commandant was always a host nation officer. In the case of AFNORTH the commandant was a Norwegian Army Colonel. He was responsible for operating the camp which included facilities, security, administration and transportation. And probably a lot more. But for official travel all we had to do was contact the motor pool and request a car and driver to pick us up at our residence and get us to the proper terminal by a specified time. They would tell us when the driver would be there, and without fail, they always were. Normally we also made arrangements to be picked up at the terminal on the return.

As requested a Norwegian military driver and sedan would be outside your front door at the appointed time. The drivers were all Norwegian Army conscripts. In Norway physically qualified males are all required to spend some time in the military. In the case of army conscripts they spend one year on active duty and many years on the reserve roster. But during their active duty period they are all snuffys — i.e. the lowest pay grade. And to compound the problem they are paid at a rate well below that of the career military. In the mid '70's that translated into something like the equivalent of 40 to 50 dollars U.S. per month. Naturally they were provided with food, clothing, medical care and quarters but spending money was pretty scarce. And when the high cost of living was factored in those meager funds bought even less. I recall talking with some of the young ladies who worked in our admin section. Two were Norwegian and one Danish. Somehow the conversation got around to their social life and the high number of unmarried males assigned to AFNORTH. One of them vividly described the situation when she said "If you date a conscript you have to bring your own money."

In any case that gives you some idea of a conscript's situation.

Back to the travel procedures. On my first official travel I managed to arrange everything properly. After calling for a car and driver a private showed up at my apartment on schedule driving an Opel, which was the smallest sedan in the motor pool inventory. That was understandable as was a LCdr at the time and among the most junior officers on the staff. Unlike a good many of the staff officers I would usually ride up front with the driver and try to converse. This was not a problem as all Norwegians are quite proficient in English having started with lessons in elementary school. On the other hand my Norsk is pitiful. But our conversations were quite fruitful in that I did get a good appreciation for the status and constraints a conscript had to endure. By far the most egregious was the low pay. We also talked about their home town, where it was located in Norway, their family etc. I also usually asked if they smoked. Nearly all did. This bewildered me somewhat as tobacco is considered a luxury in Norway and heavily taxed. Consequently any conscript who smoked probably spent nearly all of his pay on cigarettes. But they did not buy packs of cigarettes. For the most part they carried a pouch of tobacco and papers and rolled their own. This was about half the price of ready made cigarettes.

Since I was in a NATO billet I was entitled to a monthly allocation of tobacco and spirits at duty free prices. This benefit was not enjoyed by the conscripts or even the Norwegian officers who were assigned to the

Chapter XLIX

NATO staff. Being a non-smoker initially I did not bother with the tobacco allowance. But I soon began to order a carton of Prince cigarettes each month to have for friends and visitors. Prince was the most popular brand and favored by the locals. At the same time I began to start my official travel with four packs of Prince in my briefcase. I would give two packs to the driver who took me from home to the terminal and saved the other two for the driver who brought me home from the terminal on my return. The drivers were always very appreciative and on the off chance that they did not smoke the cigarettes could be used for barter.

The two packs of Prince also paid some immediate, but unanticipated dividends. Shortly after I began this practice and while I was still a LCdr, the drivers began to show up in a Mercedes. The top of the line in the motor pool inventory.

This only confirmed what I had always thought; if you treat your troops right they will do great things for you.

Chapter L

Mel

MEL WAS MORE or less a camp dog. That is to say he was not actually a battalion pet but rather the pet of whichever battalion was deployed to Camp Moscrip at Roosevelt Roads, Puerto Rico. He had been around for several years and his origin and how he got his name were a mystery. Whichever battalion was in residence became his keeper for the deployment.

But that was all right as he was quite friendly and never a problem. Well maybe he did cause a problem once but that was only as viewed by one individual. I'll get back to that later.

Mel was a mid size dog with a rather ratty looking brownish grey coat. He wasn't particularly good looking as his teeth were visible continually. Even though he was not what one would call a "junk yard dog" a first look at him might give you that impression. He may have been hit by a vehicle at some time in the past as he had a rather sideways canter. He would move in a direction that was about 15 degrees from the way his body was aligned. You might observe him walking across the area and a short time later find him right by your feet.

Whatever his shortcomings the Seabees of every Roosy battalion adopted him right away. Or perhaps he adopted the Seabees. In any case he always had food and water and plenty of Seabees to scratch his ears. And he never really seemed to play favorites. He would be around the headquarters area one day, then at the Bravo Company shops. A day or two later he would be riding around on one of Alpha company's dump trucks or watching one of the builder companies pour concrete. One of his favorite activities was to wander through the ranks while the battalion was formed for quarters. Again, he did not favor any particular company or platoon but wandered throughout the formation, including even the command group in front.

The incident that endured Mel to each and every Seabee occurred during a battalion turn over at Camp Moscrip in the early 80's.

The relieving, or incoming, battalion had sent their advance party to Moscrip to begin the turnover. All the equipment (rolling stock) and project material as well as the ongoing projects and the camp itself had to be inventoried and officially transferred to the new battalion. And it had to be accomplished in a short period of time. Consequently the inventory transfer process involved a considerable number of Seabees from both battalions. Even so, this incoming battalion had sent an unusually large number of troops on their advance party. That being the case the battalion being relieved made the grinder available to the advance party for their morning quarters.

Generally the incoming battalion has the executive officer or the operations officer as the officer-in-charge of the advance party. But for some reason this battalion assigned one of their lieutenants as the OIC. That in itself is not necessarily a problem but in this case other elements came into play. As sometimes happens when a young person is given a considerable amount of authority all at once it goes to their head. And that apparently happened in this case. Almost overnight the young officer became a martinet. He began to try to run every aspect of the turnover in spite of the fact that his advance party consisted of many chiefs and senior petty officers who had been through numerous turnovers before and knew the process in much more detail than the OIC. Never the less he began to issue "rudder orders", or detailed step by step actions for each and every turnover area. Additionally he wanted to demonstrate his new found authority by restricting the advance party personnel to the limits of the camp during the turnover. In other words no going to the base clubs after hours. To make matters worse he discovered a microphone at the podium and as too many people do he couldn't seem to stop talking. As a result the morning quarters for his advanced party would sometimes run on for half an hour or more. A normal quarters shouldn't take more than five to ten minutes. Needless to say this young officer did not endear himself to the Seabees in the advance party.

About half way through the turnover the advance party was assembled for their morning quarters and the officer was in the middle of one of his long winded diatribes on what they should do that day. The officer was full of himself while the Seabees were just hoping he would shut up so they could go to work. By this time Mel had adopted the incoming battalion so he was wandering through the ranks as usual. Eventually he shifted his sights to the command group, the other officers and chiefs in the advance party, who were formed up behind the OIC.

But he never quite reached the command group. With his sideways walk he sauntered right up to the OIC, raised his leg and peed all over his boots. The Seabees, of course, doubled up with laughter.

Mel had done what each of them would like to have done!

Thanks to RAdm Jack Buffington for reminding me of this event.

Chapter LI

Seabee Sayings

The Pentagon *a.k.a.* The big wastebasket.

Don't let your battleship mouth overload your row boat ass.

An elephant is a mouse — built to military specifications.

I know how he made Rear Admiral, I just can't figure out how he ever made jaygee.

He's so dumb he doesn't know if his asshole was drilled or punched.

Be sure to put three coats of paint on that, we need all the strength we can get.

I don't know if he's dumb or just unlucky, but I haven't got time to sort it out. Get a replacement.

The normal reward for good performance is no punishment.

I was going to join the Marine Corps, but then the recruiter found out my parents were married.

If I had known being in the Seabees was this much fun I would have joined when I was six years old. (Usually said while in the middle of a miserable task.)

Seabee dentists are called fang mechanics.

He drinks diesel fuel and craps G0-90, he must be in Alfa Company.

As-builts, ain't.

Shit flows down hill and payday is on Friday.

Even a recruit soon learns to spit on a piece of metal before he picks it up in a steelworkers shop.

We seem to be having a power problem. Get ahold of Bravo Company and have them send down more electricicals.

You ain't a builder, you're just a wood butcher.

Sonny, I've wore out more seabags than you have socks.

There I was, 10,000 feet over the barracks and not a bulldozer in sight.

Just got my liberty card so tonight I'm going out dredging for trollops.

Red sky at night, sailors delight. Red sky in the morning, sailor take warning. Seabees on the beach don't give a damn.

If that (some event) happens I'll kiss your ass on the quarterdeck, and give you half an hour to draw a crowd.

They put him so far back in the brig they had to pipe sunlight to him.

Acknowledgements

THE REALLY NICE PART of writing sea stories is that you don't have to do much in the way of research. Admittedly it is necessary to go back into the cobwebs of your mind in some instances but pure research requirements are out of the question. Bull sessions with old shipmates frequently resurrect a long ago forgotten incident and I have tried to give credit where credit is due in those instances.

Even so, I have to confess I did receive a good bit of help from various sources in the development of this collection of tales. First and foremost was the support, encouragement and patience of my wife Inger. At times I suspected that her suggestion that I go down to my basement "office" (Actually a sheet of plywood atop some sawhorses in my shop) and do some writing was only a ploy to get me out from under foot in the house. In any case she did remind me from time to time to get back to my writing and I appreciate that effort. John La Barge took a collection of old photos, cruise books, rosters etc. and came up with some recognizable reproductions for our several photos. The folks at Ag Press, Tom Carlin and Lori Daniel both made time for me in their busy schedules and helped considerably during the development process for the book. Lori spent a great deal of time working with me on the layout and formatting as well as developing the cover artwork.

The individual who deserves all manner of kudos is again Karen McVey who typed and organized my handwritten ruffs so that they came out making sense and were reasonably coherent. She was also my "sounding board" so that I could gauge how the stories would be received by the readers. At one point she told me "Many of these stories are really funny." Which pleased me greatly. Then she went on to say, "Some of that didn't actually happen, did it?" Right then I knew that at least a few of the tales were for sure class A sea stories. As I stated in the preface, they are all based on actual occurrence. How that event is described is anybody's guess.

Index

— A —

Anderson, Richard E. "Dick," 133

— B —

Barnes, George W., 107, 108, 118, 119, 183
Bartlett, James V., 120-123
Beard, John R. EO1, 52
Betts, David, 4
Binning, C. David, 180
Bodamer, Jim, 80
Bonn, Germany, 107
Bowers, Richard L. "Bowser" CM3, 90
Brandt, John C., 151
Bratland, Sverre "Jimmy," 185, 186
Braun, Richard "Charlie," 43
Brown, Harry, 4-6
Bryant, "Bear," 7
Buffington, Jack E., 192
Burr, Raymond, 85

— C —

Camp Moscrip, 191

Christchurch, New Zealand, 85
Corcoran, Tony, 62
Corzette, W.W. EOC, 90, 148
Creighton, Render, 179
Cubi Point, Philippines, 81, 161

— D —

Dairy, Glenn E. BU2, 25
Da Nang, Viet Nam, 78
Davisville, R.I., 154
DeWeese, EOC, 35
Dickey, Don, 164, 178
Diego Garcia, BIOT, 99-101, 137-140, 150
Ding Dong, interpreter, 143, 144
Dynamite, 54-57

— E —

Eddy, John, 142, 145
Elkins, John C., 110
Evans, SWC, 5

— F —

Frazier, William F. "Dick," 61

— G —
Gnader, CS2, 130-133
Goldberg, Torben, 67, 68, 107, 117
Guantanamo Bay (Gitmo) Cuba, 64, 150
Gulfport, Mississippi, 62, 96

— H —
Hartman, Frank, 89
Haynes, Howard H., 111
Hess, SWCS, 5
Hue, Viet Nam, 161
Huff, John EQCM, 150, 152
Hutton, Mike, 108

— I —
Incheon, Korea, 168
Iwakuni, Japan, 78, 81

— J —
Johnson, J.T. "Johnnie" CM3, 55, 142
Jukes – Hughes, Robin, 42

— K —
Keeling, Sam CMC, 32
King, H.L. "Doc" HM1, 122, 123

— L —
Leonard, Dan, 180, 181
Leonard, Vaughn Lea, 180
Linenberger, Tom BUCS, 164
Loberg, Pete, 17

— M —
Massy, Tom CUCM, 101
Maxwell, Ken, 134-136
MCB – One, 139
MCB – Five, 91, 167
MCB – Nine, 1, 2, 7, 13, 44-47, 80, 89, 130, 134, 167
MCB – 58, 75
McCrary, J.C. "Shot" EOCS, 32, 45, 81
Mel, 190-192
Metz, D.E. PN1, 5
Milkintas, John C., 154
Mitchell, USS, 167
Montegnards, 143-145
Moreell, Ben, xi
Mount, Jim "Doc," 46

— N —
Necas, Roger C. "Doc" HM2, 23-28, 52, 53, 90, 91, 142
Neeley, Ralph, 168
Newcomb, Frank, 94
Newton, A.W., 183
Nha Trang, Viet Nam, 90
NMCB – 62, 101, 110
NMCB – 74, 62, 164, 180

— P —
Pago Pago, American Samoa, 85
Palmerton, Leighton, 113, 116
Parker, Sam, 107
Patton, George S. Jr., 125, 136
Peffley, John Ivan "P-Fly" UT2, 28, 141-148
Peltier, E.J. "Gene," 102-105
Peredo, Vicenta C. "Seabee Betty," 109-112
Perth, West Australia, 86, 87
Peterson, "Pete" BU2, 2, 3
Phenix, Bob, 19, 21, 22
Phenix, Lucy, 19, 21, 22
Poole, A.S. "Seegar," 34-37, 57, 60, 92, 94

Port Hueneme, Calif., 54, 90, 92, 132, 133, 167
Proctor and Gamble, 28

— Q —

Quang Tri, Viet Nam, 25, 55, 90, 146, 160, 161, 170-172, 174
Quat, 27, 28
Quonset Point, R.I., 154

— R —

Reagan, Ronald, 110
Roosevelt Roads, Puerto Rico, 64, 95, 150, 190
Rota, Spain, 63
Ryan, Pete, 75

— S —

Saigon, Viet Nam, 56, 59, 92, 93, 120-122, 145, 162
Seabee Team 0809, 16
Seabee Team 0904, 132, 160
Seabee Team 7402, 4, 5
Shelton, G.M. "Marty," 154
Sigonella, Sicily, 63
Smith, J.D. EO3, 91, 92
Special Forces, 15, 24, 51, 74-77, 90, 125-129, 141-145

Sproul, Hugh, 142
Stark, Tom BU1, 165, 166
Surash, John E., 97

— T —

Tan Son Nhut, 33-36, 60, 122, 123
Tassone, Aurelio "Ray" MM1, 54
Thompson, G.L. "Tommy" CMCN, 133
Traub, "Bill," 96, 97
Tumber, Terry, 108

— W —

Walt, Lew, 89
Weaver, Glenn A., 168
Welty, A.J. "Pete" EO1, 80, 83
Werenskjold, Erik, 19
Whitfield, Dan, 27, 171
Whitman, Tom, 107
Whittaker, H. Burns, 140
Williams, J.R. "Randy," 21, 64, 65
Wright, John A. "Jack," 145, 146, 162, 163

About the Author

A. N. Olsen is a 30-year veteran of the U.S. Navy. He retired as a Captain in the Civil Engineer Corps after serving numerous command tours with the Seabees. He is a frequent contributor to Navy and engineering publications.